MY POCKET
MEDITATIONS
~FOR~
ANXIETY

ANYTIME EXERCISES TO REDUCE STRESS,
EASE WORRY, AND INVITE CALM

CARLEY CENTEN

ADAMS MEDIA

NEW YORK   LONDON   TORONTO   SYDNEY   NEW DELHI

adamsmedia

Adams Media
An Imprint of Simon & Schuster, Inc.
57 Littlefield Street
Avon, Massachusetts 02322

First Adams Media trade paperback
edition September 2020

ADAMS MEDIA and colophon are
trademarks of Simon & Schuster.

For information about special
discounts for bulk purchases,
please contact Simon & Schuster
Special Sales at 1-866-506-1949
or business@simonandschuster.com.

The Simon & Schuster Speakers
Bureau can bring authors to your
live event. For more information or
to book an event contact the Simon
& Schuster Speakers Bureau at
1-866-248-3049 or visit our website
at www.simonspeakers.com.

Interior design by Julia Jacintho
Interior images © 123RF/Ekaterina
Matveeva

Manufactured in China

10 9 8 7 6 5 4 3

Library of Congress Cataloging-in-
Publication Data
Names: Centen, Carley, author.
Title: My pocket meditations for
anxiety / Carley Centen.
Description: Avon, Massachusetts:
Adams Media, 2020. | Series: My
pocket. | Includes index.
Identifiers: LCCN 2020011409 |
ISBN 9781507213872 (pb) | ISBN
9781507213889 (ebook)
Subjects: LCSH: Stress management.
| Anxiety. | Meditation--Therapeutic
use. | Mindfulness (Psychology)
Classification: LCC RA785 .C396
2020 | DDC 155.9/042--dc23
LC record available at
https://lccn.loc.gov/2020011409

ISBN 978-1-5072-1387-2
ISBN 978-1-5072-1388-9 (ebook)

Many of the designations used
by manufacturers and sellers to
distinguish their products are
claimed as trademarks. Where
those designations appear in this
book and Simon & Schuster, Inc.,
was aware of a trademark claim, the
designations have been printed with
initial capital letters.

CONTENTS

INTRODUCTION

Are the stresses of everyday life making you feel anxious and depressed?

Do you feel uneasiness, distress, or dread before significant events?

Does worry keep you from experiencing all the good in your life?

In this chaotic and busy world, it can be difficult to cultivate a sense of calm. When you're stressed, preoccupied with worry, or anxious, relaxing can seem downright impossible. Fortunately, meditation and mindfulness can help. These practices have been shown to help ease the experiences of stress and anxiety and can help you better manage the worries you face in your life.

When you're stressed out, your mind is not focused on the moment—it's worrying about something that has happened or something that might happen in the future. *My Pocket Meditations for Anxiety* gives you 150 exercises you can do at home or at work to shut down this stress, worry, and anxiety and help you find a calm mindset that puts you back in control of your thoughts and emotions.

Meditation is an inward journey. It's personal to you, so some techniques might resonate with you more than others. The meditations and exercises in this book are designed so you can explore what techniques work best for you, whether that is guidance through visualizations, acts to focus your attention, or ways to create a sense of openness toward your thoughts.

You also don't need to do these meditations in any specific order; you can pick a chapter at random or go through them in a purposeful succession. The chapters are ordered in such a way to help you build the skills and confidence you need to progress toward stillness in your mind and body. Early chapters focus on gentle movement and visualizations designed to help you settle, and then go into meditations that calm your racing mind through your breath. Later chapters go deeper—to challenge the thinking patterns that underpin stress and anxiety, as well as to construct positive, realistic, and helpful beliefs. The final chapters provide ideas for overcoming common anxieties, bringing mindfulness into your daily life, and developing your own self-guided open awareness practice.

You can't eradicate stress from your life, but developing a healthy stress response is part of good health. The meditations in this book can ease your worries, calm your body and mind, and make you feel better prepared to handle whatever life throws your way!

PREPARING TO MEDITATE

Before you get started with meditation, it can help to understand the basics of the practice.

Some of the meditations in this book will have specific directions to lie down or move in specific ways, but for most of them the general guidance is to find a seated position in a quiet space where you can be comfortable and won't be interrupted. Before each meditation, take some time to settle in.

1. Sit in a way that is comfortable, with some back support. This could be in a chair or on the floor, perhaps sitting on a pillow so that your hips are raised and there is no pressure on your knees or legs.

2. Set a timer for the length of time that you plan to dedicate to the day's practice.

3. Close your eyes, or rest your gaze gently in front of you.

4. Notice how you feel in your mind and body.

5. Breathe in and out through your nose.

6. Stay comfy. Particularly as you begin the practice of meditation, you want to find ease in your body rather than be distracted by minor aches and tingles. If you need to shift and adjust, do so. Over time, you'll build the ability to be more still as you gain mental strength.

7. Approach your meditation with presence, openness, curiosity, and acceptance of whatever arises in you and what you experience.

8. When your meditation is done, bring some movement back into your body, perhaps wiggling your fingers and toes, slowly at first.

9. Gently open or focus your eyes, and return your awareness to the world around you.

10. Remember: If you experienced anything especially challenging in your practice, be kind to yourself. If you need more support in managing your stress and anxiety or anything painful or challenging that has come up in meditation, always talk to your doctor.

CHAPTER 1

MEDITATIONS TO MOVE INTO STILLNESS

If it were easy to calm down when you feel stressed or anxious, you would. But feeling nervous, worried, or panicked makes it difficult to even sit still, let alone meditate. That's why this first chapter begins with gentle movements that can help you physically ease into stillness. Movement encourages you to release any tension you're holding on to in your body and helps you focus your awareness on the present. These exercises can be done on their own or as a way to settle in before a longer meditation with another exercise.

RELEASE TENSION
HELD IN YOUR BODY

Stress and anxiety cause tension within your body in so many ways. You might clench your jaw, close your hands into fists, or walk with hunched shoulders. You can become so used to holding yourself in a certain way that you don't even notice the tension being held. As a result, you're not even consciously aware of how the way you feel is showing up in your body. Use this exercise to purposefully add tension to different areas of your body so that you can feel what it's like to release into a relaxed state of being.

1. Lie down somewhere comfortable.
2. Beginning at your feet, clench your toes and ankles as hard as you can as you breathe in.
3. As you breathe out, release your toes and ankles. Note how your feet feel.
4. Next, on an inhale, tense your legs, squeezing your kneecaps in and tightening your thighs.
5. Release everything on your exhale, and take a moment to register how you feel.
6. Repeat, moving up the body, tensing and releasing with your breath. Squeeze your buttocks. Contract your belly. Make fists with your hands to bring tension from your shoulders down your arms. Clench your jaw; squish your nose; squeeze your eyes.
7. Lastly, clench everything you can in your entire body as you slowly breathe in.
8. Release everything on the exhale. Notice how the tension leaves your body with your breath.

FREE YOUR NECK
FROM STRAIN

If you spend your day looking down at a device, this exercise is for you. Carrying the weight of your head forward all day can contribute to poor posture and pressure in your neck. Use this seated exercise to release tension from your neck.

1. Drop your chin toward your chest.
2. Slowly roll your head to your right side, bringing your ear over your right shoulder while keeping your shoulders down away from your ears.
3. From that same position, tip your chin *slightly* farther back and *slightly* farther forward, noticing as you do how that changes the stretch you feel in your neck.
4. Roll your head back down to your chest and over to the left side.
5. Notice the sensations in your neck, tipping your chin ever so slightly forward and backward.
6. Roll your head back down to your chest and back over to the right side. This time, pause in a place that feels like a comfortable stretch and take a full round of breath, in and out.
7. Again, roll your head back down to your chest, and repeat this held stretch on the left side with a full breath.
8. Slowly roll through in this way from one side to the other, taking a full breath at the top of each side and moving slower through the transitions than you started with.
9. After five rounds, roll your chin to your chest. Take one full breath.
10. When you're ready, lift your chin.

FOLD
AND UNFOLD

There's something deeply soothing about folding into yourself. This exercise plays with coming in and out of this sheltering feeling so that you can hold on to a feeling of safety even when you are feeling more exposed.

1. Sit tall in a chair and place your palms on your knees.
2. On an exhale, round your back forward as if you were a cat stretching, curving your shoulders forward and tucking your chin into your chest.
3. Inhale and uncurl your spine back upward to arch your back, lifting your chest upward with shoulders back and chin up.
4. Repeat, moving slowly from an arch on each inhale to a rounded back on each exhale, for five rounds of breath.
5. Return to a tall spine. Inhale.
6. Fold forward, hinging from your hips, taking your belly over your thighs as you exhale. You can let your arms hang down beside you in your chair, like a rag doll. If you're seated on the ground, crawl your fingertips out in front of you. Go as deeply forward as you feel you want to.
7. Take a full breath, and notice how safe you feel in this folded shape.
8. On your next inhale, rise back up and sit tall, taking this feeling of safety with you.
9. Repeat this folding and unfolding as many times as you need so that you can fully hold that feeling of being protected when you're sitting tall.

SIT A
LITTLE TALLER

Constant anxiety has a way of showing up in your body: You might shrink into yourself, hunch your shoulders forward, look down, and make yourself appear smaller. This exercise counteracts this effect by finding ways to lengthen the spine and sit tall.

1. Sit comfortably in a chair or on the floor with some space around you for movement. As you sit, imagine a rope is pulling you from the base of your spine up through the crown of your head, anchoring you as you find length throughout your whole back to sit taller.
2. Keep your seat steady as you shift your torso, moving from your waist to one side as if you're craning to see around something.
3. From your off-kilter position, shift your upper body forward and to the center so that you are now leaning forward with a long spine.
4. Next, take your torso to the opposite side to the one you started from.
5. From here, round your spine backward and to the center, tucking your navel and your chin in.
6. Continue this pattern of "stirring the pot," tracing the four corners like a diamond shape, for a total of five rounds.
7. Reverse the direction of your movements, and repeat for five more rounds.
8. Return to your original position of sitting tall and find length in your spine again, noticing if you can sit even taller now that you've explored a range of movement through your spine.

TEND TO
YOUR HEART

A powerful way to counter worry and anxiety is through an inner sense of courage. This exercise will help you feel a confidence in your body that can translate to your inner emotional state. This practice focuses on cultivating an inner sense of bravery through an expansion of your chest and shoulders.

1. Sit comfortably in a chair. As you begin to notice how you feel at the start of this exercise, smile softly. Throughout this practice, notice if your smile fades, and if it does, return to this small smile of peace.

2. Hold your arms out in front of you and interlace your fingers. Press your hands away from your shoulders so that your palms are facing away from you. Feel this stretch across the back of your shoulders. Release your arms back to a comfortable position.

3. Next, sitting slightly forward if you need some space behind you on your chair, interlace your fingers behind you at the base of your spine with your palms facing upward, drawing your arms down and away from your shoulders. Notice this stretch across the front of your shoulders and chest.

4. With your hands still clasped behind you, carefully raise your arms away from your body slightly, seeing how this changes the sensations across your chest.

5. Release your arms and take your hands to your hips. Remember your soft smile. Feel ready to take on what you need to with an open heart.

SHRUG
IT OFF

What you carry with you emotionally can feel like a physical burden that you are loaded down with. If your worries feel like a weight on your shoulders, try this exercise to release the heaviness from your body.

1. Squeeze your shoulders up toward your ears as you inhale through your nose.
2. Hold your breath for just a moment here at the top.
3. Quickly release your shoulders down with a fast and audible sigh out through your mouth. Let any emotional heaviness you feel release out with this sigh as the breath leaves your body.
4. Repeat several times until you feel that you have nothing emotional left to release.
5. Next, gently roll your shoulders up and back in a circular rhythm. Move slowly, feeling every part of the movement as your shoulder blades move down your back.
6. Reverse this motion, taking your shoulders up and forward.
7. As you make these circles, notice how free your shoulders are to move, working through any clicks or sticky points. Pay attention to how light your shoulders feel as they become more and more free, and how you no longer feel burdened with what you were carrying. Take this light feeling with you as you come back to stillness.

LENGTHEN
YOUR SIDES

You can get stuck in your patterns, habits, and ways of being and seeing. If you're trying to fix a problem or issue that is bothering you, it can help to look at it from a different angle. This exercise focuses on the side body—an area that is often neglected when your day involves a lot of sitting. Move in a new way and see if it helps you see a problem in a new way too.

1. On an inhale, sweep your arms up overhead.
2. At the top, take your right hand and wrap it around your left forearm.
3. On an exhale, tilt your body sideways toward the right, coming into a crescent or banana shape. Pull gently on your forearm, noticing what you feel down the left side of your body.
4. Release your arms and return to a neutral, tall spine. Pause to take a moment to observe how each side of your body feels— the stretched side compared with the nonstretched.
5. Once again, inhale and raise your arms.
6. Take your left hand and wrap it around your right forearm.
7. On an exhale, tilt to the left into a crescent shape, and explore the stretch on the right side.
8. Release your arms, and again notice how each side feels. Notice if you can now sit a little taller, having made space at your physical edges.
9. Repeat for a total of five times on each side.

TWIST
AND RELEASE

A good way to release pent-up worry is to twist your body. Twisting is a way of creating tension so that you can let it go and then recognize the aftereffects in your body. You need some space behind you for this exercise, so if you're seated in a chair, begin by sitting forward at the front edge.

1. From your seated position, inhale to sweep both arms overhead.
2. As you exhale, twist your torso to your right, lowering your right arm behind you and your left arm to the top or outer side of your right thigh. Don't pull or jerk yourself. Simply let your arms fall where your spine allows for a natural twist.
3. Inhale and see if you can comfortably find more length in your spine.
4. Exhale and deepen the twist ever so slightly.
5. Carefully take your gaze over your right shoulder if you want to go further into the twist.
6. Unravel and sit tall. Take a moment to notice how the left side of your body feels compared with your right.
7. Repeat by inhaling your arms up overhead and turning to your left as you exhale, lowering your left arm behind you and your right arm to your left thigh.
8. Lengthen your spine with your inhale and deepen the twist slightly on your exhale, gently taking your gaze over your left shoulder if you wish to go further with the twist.
9. Unravel and sit tall. Notice how you feel.

SUPPORT
YOUR HIPS

The hips are a common area to hold on to tension and tightness, especially for those who spend most of their days sitting at a desk. Let a release of this tightness be like a release of the tension and uncertainty that can come with anxiety. You may want to have a blanket handy for this exercise.

1. Come to a Low Lunge yoga pose with your right foot stepped forward in between your hands on the ground, bending your knee directly over your ankle, while your left leg slides back behind you with your left knee on the ground and toes untucked. Use a blanket underneath your left knee for some padding.
2. Rock slightly forward and back, feeling into a stretch you might receive in the front of your left hip.
3. Switch your legs and repeat by taking your left leg forward and right leg slid back with your right knee on the ground. Again, rock slightly to explore a feeling of extension in your right hip. Move comfortably out of the position.
4. Next, move to a chair and sit tall.
5. Cross your left ankle over your right thigh.
6. Fold forward from your hips as much or as little as you like, feeling where you notice any sensation in your outer left hip.
7. Switch legs, crossing your right ankle over your left thigh, and repeat this investigation of any stretch you feel in your outer right hip by folding forward.
8. Return to sitting tall.

STRETCH YOUR
WHOLE BODY

Your body is one kinetic chain—everything is connected, and taking shortcuts in one area means that you'll pay a price somewhere else. For example, lifting a heavy box by bending over from your hips and using only your back can cause pain, whereas bending your knees and recruiting the muscles of your legs is safer. It can be similar if you try to ignore your problems—you pay the price in increased stress and anxiety down the line. This exercise is a reminder of the interconnectedness of things and the support available to you.

1. Sit on the floor and stretch your legs out straight in front of you. Elevate your hips by sitting up on a pillow, or bend your knees slightly so that you can still sit tall.

2. Lengthen through your spine. You might already get a stretch along the back of your legs here.

3. Inhale your arms up overhead.

4. Exhale and fold forward over your legs. You don't need to go far—this is not about wrestling yourself into a deep stretch. It's about getting to a point where you notice a stretch along the entire back of your body, from your head and neck, down your back, through your seat, down the backs of your legs, and even into your feet. Notice the connections across the entire back of your body.

5. Inhale back to a tall seated position, and repeat this motion with your breath for five rounds.

GIVE YOUR FEET
A LITTLE LOVE

Your feet carry you throughout the day. Take a moment to stop and consider the grounding support that they provide. This little exercise for the feet sends some attention to them in gratitude, while also serving as a reminder to acknowledge the support you have to weather life's storms. Here's how to do it:

1. Sit comfortably in a chair. Pick up one foot slightly from the ground and roll circles through your ankle in one direction, then the other.
2. Return that foot to the ground.
3. Repeat with your other foot, rolling through any clicks and stickiness in each ankle.
4. Next, sit on the floor, bending your knees and drawing both feet in toward your body so that the soles of your feet come together in front of you.
5. Place your thumbs on the arches of your feet and begin to massage them.
6. As you do so, extend each foot's toes away from the other's, and pay attention to how this changes the feel of the massage on your arches.
7. Massage each toe with a gentle pull away from your foot, starting with your big toe and ending with your littlest one.
8. As you focus on your feet, consider with gratitude the places they have taken you this week. Take this feeling of being grounded and supported with you as you go on with your day.

RELAX FOR A PEACEFUL SLEEP

One of the most frustrating times to experience stress and worry is before bed. When you can't get to sleep because of a racing mind or overwhelming emotions, you might try to force yourself to sleep only to find this makes you even more worked up and further distanced from sleep. This restorative exercise can be done at bedtime to help break you out of the force-resist cycle and find relaxation.

1. Lie down on your back on the floor.
2. Hug your knees into your chest and rock gently from side to side, massaging your lower back into the ground below you. Slow down this movement, even slower than you initially started with. Let your breath also slow down as you do this.
3. Release your legs down and stretch as long as you can with your arms up over your head and your toes pointing down.
4. Relax, moving your arms to your sides again.
5. Bend your knees and plant the soles of your feet on the ground hip-width apart.
6. Sway your knees from one side to the other, again taking this slow.
7. Next, pick your feet up off the ground with your knees bent and shins parallel to the ground. If available to you, rest your feet up against a wall, and take five deep breaths here.
8. Release everything and lie down comfortably relaxed.

HOLD YOUR WHOLE
BODY IN AWARENESS

A body scan is a meditative practice used to guide your attention to the present moment and away from busy thoughts or anxiety. This exercise is not about physically moving, but about directing your focus in a way that can help prepare you for meditation. Follow these steps:

1. Sit in a comfortable position. Begin by taking your awareness to your feet. Notice the points of contact with the ground or with your body.
2. After every complete inhale and exhale, move your focus to a different body part.
3. Next, take your attention to the tops of your feet and ankles.
4. Then, shift your awareness to your shins and your knees.
5. Move on to your thighs.
6. As you become aware of your hips and your seat, take in a feeling of support where you sit.
7. Notice your belly and let it be soft, not constricted or controlled.
8. Take your attention to your chest and the rise and fall of it with your breath.
9. Be aware of how your arms hang heavy as your hands rest where they are.
10. Shift your focus to your neck. Notice any tension in your jaw and let it go. Relax your tongue in your mouth.
11. Pay attention to the space between your eyebrows, to your forehead, and finally to the top of your head.
12. Take your entire body into your awareness now.
13. Lower your chin to your chest. Take a breath. Notice how you feel.

CHAPTER 2

MEDITATIONS TO VISUALIZE NATURAL CALM

When you're under stress, your focus is often honed in on the stressor so that you can deal with it as you need to. But as a result, what you "see" can be very narrow and what you take in visually is negatively affected. Visualization is a powerful meditative tool that can help you come back to the wider view. The meditations in this chapter will encourage you to build a rich picture in your mind's eye or imagination. Doing so can feel very immersive and engaging and can help you break out of any stuck patterns or worry spirals.

GREET A NEW DAWN, A NEW DAY

If you, like many people, find yourself repeating patterns of anxiety or feeling stuck in the same cycle of reactivity, try this visualization when you need a reset or a new beginning. Forgive yourself for yesterday. Approach a new day and let the light in.

1. Imagine a dark night sky. Build up as much detail as you can in your mind's eye. Are there any stars in your sky, or clouds? If there is a moon, what phase is it in and what is the quality of its light?

2. Picture your virtual surroundings. Where are you? Are you inside looking out? Are you in nature or in a city? What is around you? Take a moment to fill in the scene surrounding you with as much specificity as you can.

3. Now return to watching the sky. Imagine the darkness is starting to dissolve and light is beginning to slip through, like a door slowly being opened. Concentrate on the quality of the emerging light. What color is it? How are the stars, moon, clouds, or other things in your scene changing as the light enters?

4. Watch everything in your scene as the sky becomes lighter and lighter. As it does, notice how your mind, too, becomes lighter and lighter.

CLEAR
OBSTACLES

Obstacles in your life can be a source of great stress and anxiety. If you ignore them and allow things to pile up around you, it can feel like a dam about to burst. Use this visualization when you need to find ways to clear the obstacles in your life so that your energy can flow freely.

1. Picture a river with as much detail as you can. How wide is the river? How fast or slow does it move? Are there trees or open space around it?
2. Envision a branch that has fallen across part of the river. See how the water slows down around it but can still pass.
3. Now imagine rocks, leaves, and other debris beginning to accumulate behind the branch. See how this further constricts the flow of the water. The original obstacle is compounded because it has not been cleared.
4. Now watch as pressure builds up behind the branch, eventually loosening it. Picture it as it drifts down the now-free stream. Notice how the water can now flow where before it was blocked. Problems or obstacles in your life that you're avoiding can be like the branch. A single issue doesn't stop you right away, but if you ignore it, it allows pressure to build and build.
5. Take a moment to watch the river flowing freely. What one simple step can you take to free up an obstacle in your life?

GLIDE LIKE THE WIND THROUGH WILDFLOWERS

A common experience during intense stress and anxiety is to feel trapped. Trapped in your body. Trapped by your racing thoughts. Trapped in your situation. This visualization can help counter a feeling of being stuck with a feeling of being free, strong, and stable.

1. View yourself standing in a field full of tall grasses and wildflowers.
2. Fill in the details around you, first by zooming out. What kind of day is it? What is the quality of the sky and the weather?
3. Start to zoom in. What is in the field to the horizon? Are there any trees, buildings, or hills? What kind of flowers are there? Notice any small insects flitting from flower to flower. Zoom in further still to a single flower, and notice its color, the delicate nature of its petals and leaves.
4. Start to walk through the field, and as you do, imagine your arms swinging by your sides. Reach down to gently feel the grasses and flowers with your fingertips as you move.
5. Watch how the wind makes the stalks gently sway and how your fingers glide with them. The wind moves through the flowers, but they remain upright and stand tall. Likewise, project that your thoughts move through you like the wind, but you stay standing tall.

BATHE IN
A FOREST

Spending time in nature is very healing. Forest bathing is the practice of getting back to nature from lives that are often dominated by concrete jungles. And because, in a sense, your brain doesn't really know what is fact and what is fiction, visualization can help you access this benefit to induce calm wherever you might be. Follow these steps to give it a try:

1. In your mind's eye, take yourself to a forest, observing what kinds of trees surround you.
2. Begin to walk through the forest, taking note of the ground and its sensation beneath your feet, whether it's soft or firm.
3. Listen to the sounds of the forest. What is the farthest thing you can hear from where you are walking? What sounds are near to you?
4. Take in the scents around you. Describe them to yourself as you identify them in your walk.
5. Imagine a space that seems inviting to lie down in. Perhaps it's a bench or a soft patch of grass in a clearing. Lie down here and look up into the canopy of the trees above you.
6. Watch the crowns of the trees reaching up into the sky. Imagine the sky above, and picture any clouds going by.
7. Breathe in and out through your nose as you watch the scene, feeling at one with the nature around you, with the space where you lie, with the trees that stretch, and with the clouds that drift.

OBSERVE THE CHANGING SEASONS

One powerful reminder to stay present is to acknowledge that everything changes. If you're dealing with chronic stress or anxiety, it can be easy to forget that even these seemingly unending feelings do shift and change in quality from moment to moment. How you feel right now—whether you judge it to be good or bad—can, and does, change. Use this visualization to meditate on the changing seasons and to remember that this, too, shall pass.

1. Call to mind a beautiful outdoor view that you love. Bring yourself to that place with as much detail as you can remember. What can you see? What does it feel like on your skin? Are there any distinct smells? What noises surround you?

2. Imagine your place in the summer. Feel the quality of aliveness, brightness, and warmth that summer holds.

3. Imagine your place in the fall. Energy is peaking and fading, beautifully preparing for a rest.

4. Imagine your place in the winter. Perhaps everything in your scene is now asleep or simply conserving energy in a dormant state, knowing that recharging requires downtime.

5. Imagine your place in the spring. Notice the calmness with which new growth begins, and the increasing momentum as buds begin to burst forth once again.

6. Consider which season you are in as you reflect on something causing you stress. Is it time to grow, release, rest, or invest?

SINK YOUR TOES
IN A SANDY BEACH

Even when the world seems like it's falling apart, can you find ways to be grounded? Can you relax and enjoy the process in all of its messiness and still feel provided for? This visualization is about yielding and allowing and yet at the same time feeling supported. Follow these steps to give it a try:

1. Picture yourself standing on a beach of fine white sand in a cove. Look out toward the water, completely clear and shallow with only small gentle waves coming into the shore protected by the curve of the land around you.
2. Mentally, curl and uncurl your toes. Feel as the sand moves to slightly cover your feet. Feel its warmth and protectiveness as a cocoon around where you stand.
3. Next, take a couple of steps into the shallow surf.
4. Each time the water drifts in toward the shore and back out again, notice that your feet sink a little deeper in the wet sand as granules are carried out from below you with the little waves.
5. Feel how you're still standing firm. You're still supported, even as the ground below you shifts and changes. The waves lap softly in. The waves softly retreat. Your feet sink and become covered in the sand, feeling cool, enveloped, and sheltered.
6. Take this feeling of calmness, of protection, and hold it in your mind, even when things around you in your life are shifting, ebbing, and flowing.

FIND SOLITUDE
IN AN OASIS

You may find yourself in a situation sometime and wish you could be anywhere else. You can't avoid stressful situations entirely, but if it's a situation that allows it, you can find calm with this visualization of a place of peace just for you.

1. Imagine yourself walking across sand dunes in a desert. The dunes sweep high all around you, the sky is cloudless, the sun hot and high. Every step shifts the sands beneath your feet.
2. As you approach the top of a hill, see below you an oasis of palm trees with a large and inviting lake.
3. Feel the breeze across your face as you take in the scene. Around you as far as you can see are hills of sand, but before you is a perfect place just for you alone to take refuge from the heat.
4. Visualize yourself running down the hill toward the lake. You can hear the sound of gently lapping water on the sandy shore as you arrive.
5. Cup your hands and fill them with water to take a refreshing drink. Step as far into the lake as you'd like to go, feeling its waters cool your entire body.
6. Emerge and sit against the support of a tree, knowing that you can return to the calming coolness of the water any time you want.

SYNC YOUR RHYTHM
WITH THE WAVES

Getting stuck in an anxious response can feel like your natural rhythm is lost. This meditation will help you sync your breathing with the endless rhythm of the ocean to bring back a sense of equilibrium in your breath and your body.

1. Become aware of your breath as you breathe in and out through your nose. Notice its quality, pace, and rhythm as the breath enters and leaves your body. Is it deep or shallow? Fast or slow?

2. In your imagination, envision yourself sitting on a shore. It might be white sand or pebbles, a large open ocean or a small bay—see where your imagination takes you, and take the time to add as much detail as you can.

3. Watch the waves coming in and out as you sit. Pay attention to their quality, pace, and consistent rhythm. Are they large and crashing or small and gentle? Fast or slow?

4. Bring your awareness to your breath while holding the rhythm of the waves in your mind. Notice the rhythms of both: In and out. In and out. In and out.

5. See if you can tune the rhythms of your breath and of the waves to match each other so that what you breathe is visually seen in your mind as a wave.

6. Begin to imagine the waves getting longer, taking your breath deeper and slower with them. Breathe with the waves.

ZOOM OUT
FOR PERSPECTIVE

One of the best ways to get a panoramic view is to climb a high mountain. If your worry and anxiety are making you see the world through a pinhole, with a narrow focus only on what is burdening you, take in an expansive view with this meditation.

1. In great detail, imagine that you have just arrived at the summit of a hill or mountain with a lookout point.
2. Take your gaze down to the lowest point you can see. Focus here for a moment as you breathe.
3. Begin to scan outward, taking your gaze up while still holding within it that low point. Notice the landscape, the trees, the vegetation, and the ways the land emerges or is obscured by features in the foreground and background.
4. Take in the expanse of the sky, again while still holding in your vision the entirety of the view you have scanned from where you stand.
5. See the scale of all the things below you. Watch how the scale grows for those things you see closer to you. Take in the smallness below. You are high above it, far from these things.
6. Consider the vastness of everything you can see. Feel the awe of these landscapes carved over centuries.
7. Hold a problem that is worrying you in your mind. Now see that problem at the bottom of your view—small and far away—as you take in the full scene.

IMAGINE
YOURSELF GROWING

You might see yourself as being more fixed and unchanging than you actually are. You could feel anxious that how you are now is how you will always be. The truth is that everything changes. Your life, your situation, and your very self are in a constant state of growth. This visualization will help you to take a step back and appreciate where you are in the continual process of becoming.

1. In your mind's eye, imagine a seed planted into the earth. Picture the way it is surrounded by dirt and darkness.
2. Shift your view to the top of the soil. Watch as the seed sprouts, punching strong through the ground. Feel the warmth of the sun on it, like the encouragement from others in your life cheering you on. Drink in the rain that nourishes it, like the resources and support you have.
3. Watch as the plant grows upward, developing a bud. Let the bud unfold. Picture the shape, the color, and the feel and texture of the petals. Even imagine the smell of the flower.
4. See the bloom change and fold into itself as the time comes to scatter its seeds and begin the cycle again.
5. Consider something that is on your mind, and ask yourself where you are in the process of growth and change. Are you protecting a seed? Feeding and nurturing a small plant? Blooming? Or preparing to begin again?

CALM A
RAGING STORM

Change, and the interior shifts you experience, can be rapid. Your swirling emotions and thoughts can be like the weather—at times stormy and difficult, and at other times calm and easy to handle. Try this meditation as a reminder that what you feel in this moment will change.

1. Notice your emotion right now. What do you feel? Put a word to this feeling.
2. Scan where this emotion is showing up in your body. How do you feel? Are there any areas of tightness, tingling, numbing, or other sensations?
3. Don't worry about controlling or changing the feeling or sensation right now. Instead, imagine in your mind a stormy, rainy day. Listen to the raindrops as they fall against a windowpane, from behind which you can watch the scene, protected in a dry interior room. Watch the drops as they fall, merging with others, trailing down the window.
4. See the rain getting lighter. As you do, imagine the emotion you feel getting lighter. The sound of the rain begins to grow fainter. The sensation of the emotion in your body grows fainter.
5. Watch the clouds begin to lighten and part, slowly revealing blue sky. Watch what you feel begin to lift and shift, revealing new feelings of peace.
6. Listen for the final drops of rain as they stop and the sky completely clears. Notice how you feel now as your emotion fades and clears to reveal something new.

CREATE A SPECIAL
SAFE PLACE

Many of the visualizations in this chapter seek to bring you to the calm of nature any time you need it. But it can be helpful to find a place that is especially meaningful for you that you associate with safe feelings of relaxation, tranquility, and peace. The more you return to this place, the stronger this association will become and the faster you will be able to access these calm feelings when you need to. Follow these steps to discover your special place:

1. Think of a place that gives you the feeling of being safe, of being at home with yourself and your thoughts.
2. Imagine this place in great detail. Are you indoors or outside? What sounds are far from you? What can you hear close by? What does it smell like? What is the quality of what you feel or what you can touch? Are there any tastes you associate with this place?
3. Picture your body feeling as comfortable in this place as it could possibly be. Sit and relax and feel supported by the place.
4. Zoom out and picture yourself where you are sitting within the scene, as if you were floating above yourself and observing yourself. See how serene and protected you are here.
5. Return to your body, taking with you the knowledge of your own special vision of safety. Know that you can return to this place, to this feeling, at any time.

LET GO WITH
THE SETTING SUN

This chapter began by greeting the new, but at times you also need to acknowledge an ending. To make space in your life for the new, you have to let go of what you no longer need. Imagine your stress and anxiety dissolving at the end of the day with this sunset visualization.

1. Hold in your mind something that you want to let go of. Don't judge whatever it is. Accept that to let go of it, you must first acknowledge that it is part of you.
2. Picture a soft blue sky where you can see the sun lowering slowly toward the horizon.
3. Hold the thing you want to let go of within your image of the sun, placing it within its light.
4. Watch now as the ball of light holding the weight of your thought sinks deeper and deeper to the edge of where you can see.
5. Notice as the colors change, becoming warmer in the sky, to pinks, oranges, and purples. The light is scattering and dissolving, and with it, what you held on to. Picture your thought sinking closer toward the horizon with the sun and the colors.
6. Watch as the sun slips faster and faster the closer it gets to the horizon. See the colors start to fade into the night sky. Notice that the thought you were holding has faded with them. You now see a canvas of stars, all of them new possibilities.

CHAPTER 3

MEDITATIONS TO UNDERSTAND STRESS AND ANXIETY

You might think of anxiety as something to get rid of. This is not only impossible, but also not the goal. Your body wonderfully evolved to respond to things that need your attention, whether it be an external threat or an internal worry. It's when stress or anxiety becomes unmanageable or never-ending that it can affect your well-being. The meditations in this chapter will help you understand what is going on in your mind and body when you're experiencing these seemingly negative things. As a result, you will know they are normal—and can even be used to your advantage in taking action or finding calm.

LISTEN TO
YOUR STRESS

If you think about stresses in your life, you might first think about the source. A demanding workload. Difficult relationships. Or even simply "life." Stress is actually a physical response in your body that kicks in to help you with extra resources that enable you to act fast. Use this exercise to begin listening to what your stress could be telling you.

1. Think about something specific that is causing you stress.
2. As you consider this person, situation, or thing, notice how you feel in your body.
3. Ask yourself the question: What is this stress telling me? It's okay if you're not sure.
4. Think about the idea that stress is actually here to help you act. Is this stress telling you that you need to take action? What one first action could you take?
5. If no action seems possible right now, think about the presence of stress as trying to help you identify a resource you need. Resources are things like time, energy, finances, support, knowledge, or anything else you require to help deal with what you need to. Do you need more resources to handle this stress? How can you take one action toward finding these resources?
6. Hold in your mind what this stress is telling you to do and what resources you need so that you can take one step toward addressing it.
7. Create a plan, and envision yourself carrying it out.
8. Notice how you feel in your body now.

SEE THE POSITIVE
SIDE OF STRESS

As far as your body is concerned, stress is not specific—it's neither good nor bad, but simply a response in your brain and body to demands that require you to act. Even the good stuff in life, such as earning a promotion or starting a new relationship, carries stress with it. Because stress tells you to act, it can be positive, motivating, and exciting. Try this meditation to reframe how you see the role of stress in your life.

1. Think about something specific that is causing you to feel stressed out.
2. Investigate how this stress is making you feel. Is it positive and motivating? Or is it negative and defeating?
3. Take a deep breath and notice the breath fill your body and then leave your body.
4. As you breathe in, imagine you are gathering with your breath the positives of what is causing you stress. Consider the opportunities within this situation and the fact that without challenge you would be bored and stagnant.
5. As you breathe out, imagine you are letting go of anything negative related to the stressor. Consider where you need support and how too much challenge could overstretch you and leave you feeling helpless.
6. Continue to inhale the good and exhale the negative as you find your balance between too much and too little.

MAKE SENSITIVITY
YOUR SUPERPOWER

Stress and anxiety can trigger similar processes in your mind and body, but they're not entirely interchangeable. Stress could be considered a response to circumstances that are often clearly identifiable and external to you, whereas anxiety is more internal and general in nature. High anxiety can make it even more difficult to handle stress. Individual factors like your level of anxiety, your experiences, your environment, and your genes influence how you experience stress. Something that might bother you a great deal might seem like only a little thing to someone else. But, as with the positive side of stress, there can be positive ways to see your anxiety too. Follow these steps to see how you can reframe your anxiety:

1. Think about something coming up that causes you to feel anxious.
2. Explore how thinking about this makes you feel in your body.
3. List in your mind any intense feelings you have related to the anxiety. Fear. Embarrassment. Worry. Dread. Judgment.
4. Next, reframe these feelings into what they positively offer you to help deal with the situation when it comes up. For example, the sensitivity that anxiety brings can make you a more intuitive person, a good listener, a deep friend, or a considered problem-solver.
5. It might help to consider when you've felt this way in the past and what you did in those circumstances. But remember that how you *feel* does not have to dictate what you *do*.

WELCOME
FIGHT OR FLIGHT

Your body has evolved to react quickly to external threats—to process that the rustling in the bushes could be a lion—so that you can decide to flee, fight it, or freeze. This is an incredibly rapid and automatic process of your central nervous system. You'll breathe faster; your heart rate and blood pressure will increase to prepare your muscles for action; and your body will produce hormones to help you focus and think. Befriend this natural response so that you can use it to your advantage rather than become immobilized by fear and feel out of control. This meditation will show you how.

1. Notice if you're in a heightened, anxious state in which you are breathing faster.
2. Identify where you are feeling fear in your body.
3. Say to yourself, "I am experiencing stress and anxiety. I am not this stress and anxiety."
4. Identify the source of your fear. Is it that you can't control the outcome you want? Or that you'll be judged by others? Or that you can't handle the situation? Dig deep into the feeling.
5. Reframe your fear and anxiety into excitement. Say to yourself, "I get to try this and see what happens. I get to show others who I am. I get to be challenged by this, and I am about to grow." Depending on the source you have identified, counter your fear with a reframed perspective.
6. Notice any changes in how your body feels.

REST
AND DIGEST

Once a perceived threat has passed, your parasympathetic nervous system helps to restore balance in your mind and body. An amazing thing about this part of your nervous system is that you can influence it through conscious processes like breathing. This means that you can help your body find balance when you're experiencing stress and anxiety. Here's how:

1. First, get into the Child's Pose yoga posture: Kneel on the floor or a bed and have two pillows nearby.
2. Place one pillow in front of you. Place the other pillow on top of your ankles and calves.
3. Sit back on the pillow on your ankles. You can have your legs together, or also try having your big toes touching and your knees wide in a V shape. Experiment with what is comfortable.
4. From this position, fold forward from your hips over the pillow in front of you, turning your head to one side. You can use another pillow or blanket to build this support higher if that feels more comfortable. Place your arms by your sides or out in front of you by the sides of the pillow.
5. Relax into the support below you.
6. Breathe without trying to control or constrict your breath, and count how long you spend on every inhale and every exhale.
7. Next, take a breath counting your natural inhale, but breathe out slowly for twice as long as your inhale. Repeat for a total of five breaths.
8. Feel protected, supported, and safe here.

GAIN CONTROL
OF CHRONIC STRESS

Although the dance of fight or flight is perfectly designed for balance, you could encounter problems if you find you're stressed out all the time. Without a counterbalancing rest, you might suffer fatigue, memory problems, and concentration trouble, among other issues. This meditation is about noticing on a minute level how things shift and change within you, even when you're highly stressed.

1. When your stress or anxiety is feeling never-ending, consciously pause and pay attention to the sensations in your body. Perhaps you're experiencing tightness in your chest, a racing in your heart, or a headache. Perhaps you don't feel anything but numb. Whatever you feel, notice it in your body.
2. Breathe in and focus closely on the feeling.
3. Breathe out and focus closely on the feeling.
4. Observe that the sensation in your body is never fully constant.
5. Take several breaths, noting the quality of the changes in the sensation, however small.
6. With your fingertips, tap the area of the body on which you are concentrating and see how that changes the quality of the sensation.
7. Just as the sensation in your body is never fully constant, neither is your stress and anxiety. Hold in your mind the movements, however small, of the stress lessening in your mind and body.

MEET YOUR
TWO MINDS

Who does the thinking in your head? You might be tempted to respond that you do, obviously. But think about this: You can have a thought, but you can also be aware of that thought. So who is doing the thinking, and who is observing? In meditation, it can be useful to think about yourself as having two minds: the one that does the thinking or narrating, and the one that watches the story being told. Sitting in meditation is a way of observing what the narrator is doing so that you can be more aware of what is going on in your mind.

1. As you sit in meditation, allow your thoughts to come and go as they arise. Watch your thoughts as if you were watching a movie in a theater.
2. Don't try to control your thoughts, to push them away, or to direct them. Simply watch what you're thinking.
3. If you start to get caught up in a particular train of thought, bring your focus back outward to the movie theater and view your unfolding stories on the screen.
4. Just like when you are at the movies, you can be aware of the content of the story playing out while being at a distance from the story. It is both real and unreal. You might feel certain things about your thoughts or as a result of them, but try to hold them from an observer's distant perspective.

TAME
YOUR MIND

Simply observing your thoughts is harder than it sounds! The problem you might encounter with your "two minds" is that you may have come to overly identify with your narrating mind. You might think every thought is true. You could think every thought is "you." The truth is, thoughts happen. As you watch them, you'll start to notice how random they are, how repetitive they are, and how not all of them are true. But the narrating mind is greedy for your attention and pulls you around. It's why it's often called your "monkey mind." It's like a chimp tearing around, swinging from branch to branch. What's the best way to tame a monkey? Give it something to do. The same concept applies to your mind, which is the aim of this meditation.

1. As you observe your thoughts and become distracted by them, bring your attention to your breath as a focal point.
2. With every inhale, say to yourself, "I am breathing in."
3. With every exhale, say to yourself, "I am breathing out."
4. Repeat for five slow breaths.
5. Return to observing your thoughts.
6. Come back to your breath every time you find yourself getting overly caught up in your train of thought.

TRAIN
YOUR MIND

It can feel frustrating when your "monkey mind" continues to run around during meditation. But don't think of it as failing every time you find yourself needing to redirect your attention back. In fact, you're building strength every time you notice you're caught up in your thoughts and you guide your awareness out of them. When training for a marathon, a runner begins with short, focused distances. As the runner's endurance builds, the training distance extends. In building your meditation practice, you're putting your mind through a short workout, bringing it back to a focal point, before getting to a stage where you can let it run free for longer.

1. Imagine a kite on a string drifting in the sky.
2. Bring your focus to your breath, saying "I am breathing in" with every inhale and "I am breathing out" with every exhale.
3. Picture the kite swaying back and forth with your breath. Watch the kite float farther and farther out as you breathe undistracted.
4. Whenever your attention wanders from your focus on your breath, simply guide it back to "I am breathing in" and "I am breathing out." Every time you find yourself caught up in your thoughts, reel the kite in a bit. With time, your mind—your kite—will cover greater distances uninhibited.

MAKE A BRIDGE
WITH YOUR BREATH

Your stress response is a process that occurs in both your body and your mind, but there's often an idea that anxiety and stress are all in your head. This might even lead you to feel trapped in your thoughts and unaware of your bodily experience of stress altogether. Your breath is a bridge between your mind and body, and consciously creating this connection can help you address the physical and mental effects of stress as one whole being. Try this exercise to see this connection in action:

1. Sit on the floor with your legs bent and feet planted on the ground. Pull your knees in a little toward your chest.
2. Take your belly toward your thighs and hug your legs, wrapping your arms around the backs of your thighs.
3. Lower your head to your knees to a comfortable position, curling inward and taking your focus inward.
4. Notice how you feel in this protective shape.
5. Take your focus to your breath.
6. Imagine yourself in this curled shape as a bridge. As you breathe, imagine sending your breath across this bridge.
7. Breathe here for as long as is comfortable in your meditation session, focusing on your breath and the way you can send it throughout your body. Whenever any distracting thoughts arise, come back to this vision of your breath as a bridge to your body.

ALLOW YOURSELF
TO WORRY

Our minds are pattern-making machines, because patterns save time and energy. But over time, if you are constantly fretting, you might find your thoughts always circling around patterns of intense worry and anxiety. One way to start managing the cycle is to set boundaries to it. This can help you compartmentalize the experience and habit of your worry so that it is not always the focus of your mind.

1. Set aside a daily time for a meditation focused solely on your worries.
2. During this time, let yourself worry about anything that you want to.
3. As a specific concern arises, follow it. Ask yourself what the worst-case scenario is if your worst fears come true. Ask yourself how likely this scenario is. Ask yourself what you'll do if it happens. Finally, ask yourself what you can do now to try to achieve a better result.
4. As you prepare to leave your worry time, let go of the worries you were focused on. Bring with you any actions you plan to take.
5. In your daily life, when a worrying thought arises, tell yourself that it is okay that you're worried, but that you'll think about it later when you have your scheduled worry time.

CHANGE
YOUR MIND

One of the most fascinating and hopeful things for you to recognize about your physical body is that your brain is remarkably adaptable. It changes based on what you feed it—what you take in, what you focus on, and what you consciously practice. This plasticity means you can adapt and change your brain through focused practice in meditation. The first step is to become aware of your thoughts.

1. Find some paper or a journal and a pen.
2. Before you begin a meditation, write down how stressed or anxious you feel on a scale of one to five, with five being most stressed.
3. After meditation, write down any thought patterns that took your focus today.
4. Over time, identify the consistent thoughts that come up for you repeatedly. Notice if you are often replaying things from the past or worrying about the future or becoming stuck in negative thoughts.
5. Outside of meditation, be mindful of the times when these patterns come up. The more you identify and become aware of your thoughts, the more you'll notice the common attributes of what you think about. Then you can start to pinpoint any negative patterns that you want to watch out for and change.

CHAPTER 4

MEDITATIONS TO RELAX THROUGH YOUR BREATH

Breathing exercises, such as taking longer exhales compared with your inhales, are one of the fastest ways you can relax your mind and body. Your breath is one of the few processes you have both automatic and conscious control over, and it influences your physical stress response and nervous system. It is also a powerful focus for staying present. Think of your breath as a present-only focal point—it's impossible to breathe in the past or the future. The exercises in this chapter start with discovering your natural breath and build up to different ways of directing your breath to find stillness.

NOTICE YOUR NATURAL RHYTHM

When you're anxious or stressed, you'll often breathe more into your chest than your belly. The first step to finding relaxation through your breath is to simply notice how you naturally breathe.

1. Focus on the breath as it enters your nostrils and as it leaves, perhaps noticing the coolness of the breath with your inhale and the slightly warmer nature of the breath on your exhale.
2. Take your hands to your belly.
3. Inhale and exhale for one full round of breath through your nose. Don't try to control your breath in any way; simply watch one breath and observe where the breath moves in your belly. This might be a large movement or it might be very small and subtle. There is no right or wrong here.
4. Move your hands to your chest. Feel the rise and fall as you breathe in and out for one count.
5. Finally, place your hands on your collarbone. Notice where the breath moves here.
6. Now rest your hands wherever they feel comfortable.
7. Take your whole body into your awareness now and feel where the breath moves in your body. If your attention wanders in your meditation, keep returning it to this awareness of the rises and falls in your body that come with your breath.

UNITE BREATH AND MOVEMENT

Your first instinct on becoming aware of your breath might be to try to control it. It's funny that sometimes when you pay attention to something, it's difficult to figure out what you normally do without thinking. To get used to observing your breath, sync it with some basic movements to help counter the impulse to control how you breathe.

1. Sit in a comfortable position and take a moment to tune in to your natural breath.
2. As you inhale, raise your arms straight out to your sides and sweep them up overhead as if you're drawing a bubble around yourself.
3. Exhale and lower your arms to your sides.
4. Keep moving in this way with your breath for five breaths. Try to match the movement to your breath on your inhale so that your fingertips just touch over your head as you finish breathing in, and match your exhale so that your fingertips reach your sides at the end of breathing out.
5. Keep moving in this way for an additional five breaths; for these breaths, incorporate your neck in the movement as well, looking up as you inhale and sweep your arms up, and taking your chin to your chest as you float your arms down by your sides, syncing both movements with your breath.
6. Pause at the bottom of your final round for a moment.
7. Lift your chin and sit tall. Notice the natural rhythm of your breath.

TAKE A
DEEP BREATH

When you are stressed, it's a common tendency to take shorter, shallower breaths as your fight-or-flight response prepares your mind and body for action. You might feel like your heart is racing when you get into a particularly anxious state and feel out of control or panicked. Try taking some deep breaths to remind yourself and your body that you are safe and don't need to work so hard at this moment.

1. Begin by becoming aware of how you are breathing right now. Is your breath short and shallow? Or is it deep and long? Is it mainly within your chest? Or is your belly moving too?
2. On an inhale, count to four to yourself and breathe in for these 4 seconds.
3. On an exhale, count to 4 seconds to yourself as you breathe out.
4. Repeat these counts to 4 seconds for five rounds of breath in total.
5. Let your breath become natural again. Don't try to control it in any way. Notice its quality and whether it is similar to when you started, or different.
6. Repeat this exercise if you still feel any panic or if you're breathing fast. If it's comfortable for you, try increasing the time for each inhale and exhale to 5 or 6 seconds.

DIRECT YOUR BREATH
TO WHERE IT'S NEEDED

One way of addressing a tendency to breathe into your chest when you're experiencing anxiety is to play with directing your breath consciously. This little meditation will help you see how it feels to breathe into different parts of your body as compared with your own natural breathing habits.

1. Take one hand to your belly and one hand to your chest with your fingertips resting on your collarbone.
2. Notice where your natural breath moves within your body as you inhale and where it leaves your body as you exhale.
3. On an inhale, direct as much of your breath as you can into your collarbone and feel how this expands your chest. Exhale.
4. On your next inhale, send your breath to your chest, feeling it rise and then fall as you exhale.
5. On your next inhale, fill your belly as much as you can with the breath you take in. Let your belly relax and be soft as you do this, resisting any urge to hold your stomach in.
6. Now notice your natural breath again. Where does the breath move when you are not consciously directing it—in your collarbone, chest, or belly?

SIGNAL SAFETY FROM
YOUR DIAPHRAGM

Taking full breaths that fully engage your diaphragm can soothe your stress response. The diaphragm, a key breathing muscle, flattens and stretches as you breathe in. The process of taking in breath is actually more about the difference in pressure that is created within you, compared with the atmosphere around you, than about trying or straining to suck in air. A vacuum effect draws in the air due to the change in pressure. This effect is why some people say that you create the space in your body and the universe fills it.

1. Check in with your natural breath and note its rhythm, pace, and depth.
2. Take one hand to your belly and one hand to your chest and collarbone.
3. Inhale and first send as much breath as you can to your belly, then fill your chest, and finally expand your collarbone, as if you were filling a glass from the bottom up.
4. Exhale and first release the breath in your collarbone, followed by the breath in your chest, and finally empty your belly of breath.
5. Repeat this three-part diaphragmatic breath for a total of five times. Remember that breathing is automatic. You don't need to strain to take in air, as if you were sucking through a straw. Focus instead on making space in each of the three areas of your body, allowing the universe to fill that space.

EXTEND YOUR
EXHALES FOR CALM

If you're in a position to relax, you can take your time. Taking longer on your exhales than on your inhales is one of the best ways to quickly calm the communication between your brain and body when you're anxious. Try this exercise:

1. First, become aware of your natural breath, breathing in through your nose and out through your nose. Check in with how you're feeling.
2. Take a deep cleansing breath, breathing in to a count of 4 seconds, and out to a count of 4 seconds.
3. On your next breath, breathe in for a count of 4 seconds, and out for a longer count of 5 seconds.
4. On your next inhale, count to 4 seconds, and on your exhale, count to 6 seconds.
5. If that is comfortable for you and you aren't straining or gasping for your next inhale by the end of 6 seconds, inhale for 4 seconds and exhale to a count of 7 seconds.
6. Again, only if that feels okay for you, inhale to a count of 4 seconds and exhale to a count of 8 seconds.
7. Stay at this level—with your exhales twice as long as your inhales (or at whichever level you are working comfortably)—for a total of five rounds, counting each round on one hand with your fingers.
8. Let your breath return to its natural rhythm. Notice how you feel.

BOX
YOUR BREATH

You might think of your breath as having two parts: an inhale as you breathe in and an exhale as you breathe out. But a full breath cycle actually consists of four parts: the inhale, a pause and turn, the exhale, and a pause and turn. Even if the pause points are very short, they represent the transition between your inhales and exhales. Box breathing is a common method that brings focus to all four parts of your breath to help you access a peaceful state. Give it a try with these steps:

1. Notice your natural breath.
2. Begin to notice how your breath is not simply an inhale and an exhale. Focus on each moment of a full breath: your inhale, the turn at the top of your inhale, your exhale, and the turn at the bottom of your exhale.
3. Slow down the pause points in your transitions between inhaling and exhaling so that you can sense each of the four parts. Don't rush through the turns.
4. Notice how the breath moves in your body during each of the four parts: Inhale. Turn. Exhale. Turn.
5. Continue to notice the four parts of your breath for five full breath cycles, naming the parts in your mind as you do. Inhale. Turn. Exhale. Turn.

LEVEL UP YOUR
BOX BREATH

Once you get used to paying attention to the four parts of the breath (see the previous exercise), you can begin to play with elongating the pauses between inhaling and exhaling. Combine this with a lengthened exhale as well and discover whether this method is an effective one for you to quickly come to a more rejuvenated state of mind.

1. Begin by noticing the four parts of your natural breath. The inhale. The pause and turn at the top of the inhale. The exhale. The pause and turn at the bottom of the exhale.

2. Start to lengthen the turning points of your breath: Breathe in for a count of 4 seconds. Retain your breath for a count of 2 seconds. Exhale for a count of 4 seconds. Pause with your body emptied of your breath for 2 seconds.

3. Repeat this four-part breath with a pause of 4 seconds to match your inhales and a pause of 4 seconds to match your exhales as well. Complete five full cycles of breath in this way.

4. Only if this feels comfortable, begin to lengthen your exhale: Breathe in for a count of 4 seconds. Pause for a count of 4 seconds. Breath out for a count of 6 seconds. Pause for a count of 4 seconds. Complete five full cycles of breath in this way; again, only if it feels okay for you.

5. Notice how you feel in your mind and body.

USE YOUR BREATH
AS A FOCAL POINT

As you get used to self-guided meditation, you might find that your breath is a helpful focal point to return to whenever your mind wanders. The more you build this up as a habit, the more you will be able to call this practice to mind wherever you are, whenever stressful or anxious thoughts might happen. To use your breath as a focal point, follow these steps:

1. Take your focus inward as you begin your meditation, noticing your thoughts as they come and go.

2. Once you are settled in, begin to take your awareness to your breath as it goes in and out of your nose. Notice the breath at the edge of your nose as you inhale and as you exhale. Perhaps the breath is noticeably cool as it enters your nostrils and warmer as it exits.

3. Be curious and investigate where the breath moves in your body. Begin from your nose and notice any small movement of your head and shoulders as you breathe.

4. Next, travel downward with your awareness, paying attention to how your breath moves in your chest and belly.

5. Finally, observe any subtle shifts in your hips, your seat, and your legs with every in-breath and out-breath.

6. Take your full body into awareness now, noticing every part of you that moves as you take in breath and as you breathe it out.

BLOCK IT
ALL OUT

If you find yourself needing a sensory break, this practice can be a powerful way to bring yourself into your body and shut out everything external. In this exercise, your senses are symbolically closed off, so that all that remains are your breath and your internal world.

1. Take a breath in, and as you exhale, begin to hum to yourself, "Hmmmmm..." Notice if this causes any vibrations within you, perhaps through your teeth or in your head.
2. Now, lift your hands with your palms facing you.
3. Place your pinky fingers under your bottom lip.
4. Place your next fingers—your ring fingers—above your top lip and under your nose, but don't block off your nostrils.
5. Lay your middle fingers under your eyes.
6. Press your thumbs lightly onto the cartilage space just in front of your ears.
7. Finally, close your eyes and place your index fingers on top of your eyelids gently.
8. Inhale, and on your exhale, hum to yourself. Notice how this feels throughout your body, with your senses now "closed."
9. Repeat, humming with every exhale, for a total of five rounds of breath.

BALANCE
YOUR BREATH

This exercise of alternative nostril breathing can be a divisive one. For some, this is an exercise that can bring clarity and calm when under stress, but for others it can increase feelings of anxiety as if you can't get enough breath into your body. With an open mind, experiment, explore, and find what works best for you. There is no right or wrong way to do this—just make sure to always listen to yourself.

1. Take your right hand and curl in your two longest fingers, while keeping your little pinky, ring finger, and thumb extended. You can relax your left hand and arm however is comfortable.
2. Press your right thumb to close off your right nostril and inhale through your left nostril.
3. At the top of your inhale, release your thumb and press your two small fingers to close off your left nostril gently.
4. Exhale through your right nostril.
5. Keeping your two fingers on your left nostril, inhale in through your right side.
6. At the top of this inhale, release your fingers and use your thumb to close your right nostril.
7. Exhale through your left side.
8. Repeat, alternately closing each side at the top of your inhales for several rounds of breath. Stop if you ever feel light-headed or anxious about your breathing.
9. Finish with an exhalation through your left side. Notice how you feel.

BREATHE
LIKE A LION

This exercise is a great release that can be especially fun for children to practice and explore the relationship between their mind, body, and breath. When you feel strong emotions associated with stress and anxiety, you don't always have an easy outlet for these intense feelings. This practice can help to powerfully release the breath and, with it, the energy attached to those difficult emotions.

1. Breathe in and out through your nose as usual; become aware of your natural breath. Notice how you're feeling and where in your body you feel any related sensations.
2. Take in a deep breath to a count of 4 seconds.
3. Pause at the top of your inhale for 4 seconds.
4. Now, quickly exhale through your mouth, opening your mouth as you do so, and sticking out your tongue as if you were a big cat. As you expel your breath, do this with an audible sigh.
5. Repeat, and make your sigh even louder on your next exhale. Don't be shy with this exercise—let it out!
6. As you sigh, release any tension or strong feelings with it.
7. Repeat for several rounds of breath until you feel more relaxed.
8. Investigate how you feel now.

CHAPTER 5

MEDITATIONS TO FIND FOCUS WITH A MANTRA OR PHRASE

If you're too caught up in stressed or anxious thoughts during meditation, a mantra can help you settle your mind on a focal point. A mantra is a simple word, phrase, or sound that you can bring your attention to if your mind wanders. The word *mantra* comes from Sanskrit, and your mantra might have spiritual significance or could be something personal just to you. It can also be an affirmation that focuses you on what you want to cultivate within yourself and your life. Try the mantras in this chapter to concentrate and calm a busy, overthinking mind.

FEEL THE
VIBRATION OF SOUND

Singing and chanting are common practices in many cultures going back thousands of years. Whether on your own or in a group, the energy you create and experience through sound can feel powerfully connecting. If you're struggling to anchor your mind on a single word or phrase, begin by exploring this active production of sound to feel more grounded.

1. Pay close attention to the sound of your breath as it enters your nostrils and as it leaves your nostrils.
2. Take a deep cleansing breath, inhaling for a count of 4 seconds, and exhaling for a count of 4 seconds.
3. Take a deep breath in.
4. Exhale slowly through your mouth, creating a sound of "om" from deep within your throat as you do so. Om is made up of three different sounds. Begin with an "ah," transition to "oh," and end by closing your lips and saying "mm."
5. Repeat this chant of om for several rounds, noticing the quality of the sound as you try to deepen it further in your throat and feeling the subtle vibrations it might create in your vocal cords, your jaw, your lips, and your teeth.
6. If your focus wanders in meditation, bring it back to stillness by repeating three rounds of om.
7. Try this exercise with a partner or a group, sitting close together to feel the sound waves mingling together and surrounding you like a protective blanket.

ASSOCIATE A SOUND WITH SOOTHING

When you first start meditating, it can be very difficult to settle your mind and body. One way to enter stillness faster is to create a routine that over time you will associate with meditation. In addition to setting aside a specific time and place that you dedicate to your practice, you can begin your meditation with this soothing sound ritual so that eventually your mind and body will more easily recognize that it is time to relax.

1. Become aware of your breath as you settle into meditation.
2. Inhale through your nose.
3. Exhale through your mouth, and as you do so, say to yourself out loud: "Ah-hum." This is an easy two-syllable tone that you can use as a settling sound for your meditation. You could also think of a sound or phrase that is more personal and meaningful to you. The important thing is to choose something that you stick with and that is unique to your meditation time rather than associated with other activities in your life.
4. Repeat your settling sound out loud with every exhale from your mouth for a total of five times.
5. Then, begin breathing in and out through your nose.
6. Repeat your settling sound *silently* in your mind with every breath for a total of five times.
7. Return to this settling sound in your mind if you find yourself getting caught up in your thoughts at any point in your meditation.

RECEIVE THE RHYTHM
OF YOUR HEART

When you're anxious or stressed, it might feel like you need something external to help you calm down. But the beat of your heart is a rhythm inside of you that can serve as a reminder that what you need starts from within. See the power of what is already within you and access this amazing gift that is always available to you.

1. Take the two fingers next to your thumb—your "peace" fingers—to your wrist or neck and find your pulse.
2. Breathe in and out, noticing the sensation beneath your fingertips. Resist any urge to control your breath or change it as you feel the pace of your pulse, but notice if your pulse changes with your breath as you settle in.
3. Feel how your pulse rises and drops under your fingertips. Recognize the subtle difference between these two parts. Observe the constant rhythm.
4. With every ba-boom of your heartbeat, think to yourself: "I am."
5. After several breaths, rest your hands wherever they feel comfortable.
6. Focus your mind on the mantra of "I am" if your attention wanders in your meditation, coming back to this simple phrase that connects you to what is within you and the life that flows through you.

KNOW THAT
YOU ARE ENOUGH

Your thoughts can play like a closed loop, and you might not even be consciously aware of how unhelpful and repetitive they are. A meaningful and positive phrase can be a great way to counter the negative self-talk that can make it difficult for you to deal with the anxiety in your life. If you struggle with internal messages that you are unworthy or not good enough, come to this meditation as a starting point for your self-inquiry. This isn't to say that there is nothing you would want to change about yourself, but seeing yourself as enough, exactly as you are now, is necessary to help you heal past wounds that could be limiting your growth. Here's how to do it:

1. Consider a part of you—or something in your life—that makes you feel like you've fallen short. What in your life makes you feel unworthy of care and attention? When do you feel "not good enough"?
2. Investigate any physical sensations in your body that come up as you focus on this.
3. Imagine that a friend told you about this feeling and where it comes from. What would you say to that friend? Treat yourself as you would a friend in need of help.
4. Say to yourself: "I am enough."
5. Repeat this mantra as you breathe, sending this thought to any places in your body where you feel any sense of unworthiness.

TELL YOUR BODY
YOU ARE SAFE

You can know logically that you are safe and sound in a given moment, but if you're in an anxious state you can feel anything but safe. It's possible you don't feel at home even in your own body. Underneath any intense emotions could be a lurking belief that you are not allowed to feel what you feel or to express those feelings. These emotions can be powerful, but to get to a point of being able to name them and experience them, you need to feel safe to do so. Create a loving space within yourself by first telling your body you are secure. Here's how:

1. Take note of any feelings of being unsafe or of being not okay that arise in your meditation.
2. Scan your body for any places these feelings manifest in physical sensations. These could include tightness in your chest, a lump in your throat, or a defensive posture you take.
3. Think of an event or time that made you feel safe. Perhaps it was with a specific person or in a specific location. Remember as many details of how you felt as you can.
4. Say this affirmation in your mind: "I am safe."
5. Breathe deeply, and repeat this mantra to yourself, holding on to the feeling of safety in your memory and sending this energy to anywhere that you feel unsafe in your body.

SURRENDER
TO SUPPORT

Perhaps you cope with intense feelings of stress and anxiety by cutting yourself off from these emotions. You might put up barriers around what you allow yourself to feel, or think you are a burden if you can't handle things on your own. Avoidance is a common survival strategy to block out or evade difficult emotions. But this tactic also walls you off from the beautiful things that are possible in life, because the barriers you erect can't tell the difference between the good and the bad. With this exercise, you can take down your walls and accept the support available to you.

1. Become aware of the ground or chair where you sit, noticing the points of contact between your body and the support below you. Allow yourself to feel held up by these supports.
2. Take this feeling of being supported and think of someone in your life whom you have helped in the past. Remember what you offered them and how they responded.
3. Move this sense of support inward to yourself, calling to mind a time you felt supported by someone else. Say to yourself, "I am supported."
4. Think of one small thing you could help someone with or something you could use help with, and make a commitment to reach out for this.
5. Come back to the mantra "I am supported" if your mind wanders during the rest of your meditation, reminding yourself you don't have to go it alone.

GROUND YOURSELF
IN THE PRESENT

If you're always worrying about the worst that could happen, you can't really enjoy what you have. Whether they include a fear of losing your job, a health concern, or the thought of never finding the relationship you desire, these worries take you out of the present. Kahlil Gibran wrote about this never-ending suffering, saying, "Is not dread of thirst when your well is full, the thirst that is unquenchable?" Ground yourself with this meditative reminder that you are provided for, no matter what challenges may lie ahead.

1. Think about something you worry could happen that would make you feel unsafe, insecure, or scared about how you would cope.
2. As you hold this idea in your mind, scan your body to see where thinking about this negative possibility shows up within you. Are you clenching your jaw? Furrowing your brow? Holding your breath?
3. Consider next what you have in the present moment. Recognize that the thing you worry about is not here currently. Feel safe, secure, and capable in the here and now.
4. Investigate whether thinking about the present situation in comparison with the future changes how you feel in your body.
5. Internalize this affirmation: "I am provided for." Return to this thought if your mind wanders in the remainder of your meditation. Be sure you don't discount what you have already due to fear about the future. Know that whatever happens, you have the power to deal with it.

BANISH SELF-PITY
THROUGH GRATITUDE

It might seem like a small act to acknowledge what you're grateful for each day, but what this does is help you see the good in everything you encounter. Over time, you start to approach your day-to-day experiences asking yourself: Is this what I'll be most grateful for today? You'll see opportunity instead of negativity when you make a commitment to this exercise.

1. Take out your meditation journal or some paper and a pen.
2. Take an inventory of anything in your life that stirs feelings of self-pity or thoughts that things are not fair. Don't judge these things, but simply get them down on the page.
3. At the end of this day, and every day going forward, write down three things you are most grateful for. Make these things as specific as possible.
4. Say this mantra to yourself in your meditation practice: "I am grateful." Note that this isn't about pretending the difficulties you face aren't real. It is, however, about challenging negative clinging and feelings of entitlement with a realistic picture and recognition for what you *do* have.
5. At weekly or monthly intervals, check back on your gratitude journaling and your initial inventory. Revisit the things you previously felt were unfair or where you felt sorry for yourself and take stock of these feelings and their impact on you now. Notice if you are more attuned to things in your life that make you happy.

CONNECT THROUGH LOVING-KINDNESS

Meditation is an opportunity to go within yourself, something that you might not often get to do because of the busyness of modern life. But don't mistake this act of self-inquiry as only an internal practice. Everything you do is in relationship, whether to yourself, to others, or to your environment. You are a connected being. Without connection, you cannot thrive. Feeling isolated and alone can compound the stress and anxiety that you feel. Reconnect both to yourself and to a sense of the interconnectedness of everything that you are a part of with this meditation.

1. Use this phrase as your mantra in your meditation: "I am connected."
2. Hold this wish for yourself as you tune in to your breath, fostering a sense of connection between your mind and your body.
3. Next, think of someone in your life who is close to you and whom you see often. Radiate the feeling of connection toward them.
4. Move this bonding energy further outward. Think of someone you occasionally see, and send them this feeling of warmth and attachment.
5. Picture a street that you go down often, full of strangers you don't know. Say to yourself and to them as they pass by: "We are connected."
6. Radiate the feeling of being connected from within yourself out to the wider world and everything in it.

RECOGNIZE WHAT'S IN YOUR CONTROL

Stress and anxiety have a way of making you feel incapable of even the most basic things. There are two ways to think about your capabilities. You can see things as completely within your influence or as completely out of your hands. More often than not, however, life requires a balanced and realistic view of both aspects. For example, you can control the effort you put into making dinner for your family, but you can't control whether they enjoy it. This meditation can help you find the balance you need to take responsibility only for what you can control.

1. Meditate on a situation that makes you feel out of your depth, or on something you'd like to do but hold yourself back from doing because you think you can't accomplish it.

2. Consider the following questions: Do you feel personally capable of doing this thing? What factors in the situation or environment are outside of your control?

3. Notice if you have a bias toward feeling everything is your responsibility or everything is out of your hands.

4. Make a plan around what is in your control and the next actionable step you can take toward what you want to do. This could be the process, the effort, the action, or the perspective you take. Let go of a focus on the outcome and the things you can't control.

5. Affirm to yourself: "I am capable."

BUILD RESILIENCE BEFORE YOU NEED IT

Resilience is a skill that you call on when things go wrong. But while resilience is needed when you face adversity, it isn't only *built* in these moments. Resilience can be cultivated when times are good so that you have what you need to recover when they're not. There are many aspects to resilience, including your community of support and the resources you have access to. There are also skills within yourself that you can train in times of safety for greater resilience in times of stress or anxiety, including an ability to learn from both the positive and the negative things you experience.

1. Recall a time in your past when you faced some difficulty outside of your control, when you felt powerless, or when things seemingly fell apart.
2. Check within your body if this memory leads to any physical sensations, any tightness, or any constriction.
3. Breathe into these spaces in your body as you ask yourself the following questions: What did I learn from the experience? What meaning did I draw from the experience that I carry forward now? In what way did that experience shape who I am now?
4. Take for yourself this mantra: "I am resilient." Repeat it to yourself if you find yourself ruminating on your negative thoughts in meditation. Focus on the lessons you've learned and the ways the experiences you've faced have made you who you are and brought you to where you are now.

SEE AND
UNDERSTAND LOVE

In spite of the fact that you can be more connected to others now than ever before thanks to social media, a common source of societal anxiety stems from a deep sense of disconnection and loneliness. One of the biggest factors in a happy life is satisfaction with your relationships. Sitting isolated behind a screen can be a poor proxy for the intimacy and closeness that you need in order to thrive. Let love build within you through this meditation, radiating a feeling of unconditional care and affection to a loved one and then turning it inward to yourself.

1. Decide on someone in your life whom you want to concentrate on in this meditation.
2. Holding this person in your mind, consider the following two facets that need to be true in order to genuinely hold them in love.
3. See who they really are; see behind any masks to their authentic truth. Without this perspective, you can't truly love, because you only love the facade instead of what is really there.
4. Understand what you see without judgment. Without this understanding, you are rejecting what is real and true, which can't be the foundation of love.
5. Think next of yourself and the love you give yourself. Ask yourself if you are loving what is authentically true within you and holding it with understanding.
6. Meditate on this mantra: "I am loving. I am loved."

BE
FREE

Imagine what it would feel like to be free from the constant grip of anxious feelings. You'll never be able to entirely remove stress and difficult emotions from your life experiences, but there is freedom to be gained in becoming a master over them, rather than allowing them to master you. A measure of control found in what you are in charge of—namely, what you believe, how you see things, and what you choose to do—can bring a sense of freedom. Follow these steps to give it a try:

1. Pay attention to whether the thoughts that come to you in your meditation are focused on the past, the present, or the future.
2. Note where these thoughts are located in these time frames—and acknowledge it. You might say something like the following: "Interesting. My mind is currently thinking about something that already happened."
3. Identify any emotions or feelings associated with the thought. Note this observation with curiosity as if it were a visitor. Rather than saying to yourself, "I am sad," say to yourself something like, "Sadness is here."
4. Release the thought and the feeling with these observations. Notice how they shift when you acknowledge them and allow them to pass.
5. As you do this, notice if it becomes any easier to bring yourself back to the present moment and focus on your meditation. Bring your attention to the mantra "I am free" whenever this thought or feeling resurfaces.

CHAPTER 6

MEDITATIONS TO GET OUT OF YOUR HEAD AND INTO YOUR SENSES

Before you can work on your relationship with what is, you need to see what is with clarity. Being mindful through your senses can help you sort through your anxious thoughts and feelings. It's via your senses that you take in information about the world and communicate. Your physical senses are like translators between your internal experience, your body, and your mind. Using the meditations in this chapter can help you tune in to these signals and develop a sense of safety within your physical body before you begin to work on the deeper levels of emotional safety later in this book.

AWAKEN YOUR
FIVE SENSES

The senses that you're probably most familiar with are sight, hearing, smell, taste, and touch. It can be easy to take these rich experiences for granted as you rush through a busy day or become distracted by the stress and anxiety in your life. Redevelop an appreciation for the subtle sensations of each of your basic five senses through this meditation.

1. Take in as wide of a view as possible of the place where you sit. Without moving your eyes around the space, observe everything at the edges of your vision. Start to narrow this focus by concentrating on what is straight ahead. Lower your gaze in front of you. Close your eyes and "look" into the back of your eyelids.

2. Listen for the sounds around you. Pick out individual noises and register if they're near to you or far away.

3. Notice the sound of your breath in your nostrils as you breathe. As you sit here, take note of anything you can smell, separating out any specific scents from one another.

4. Focus on your tongue in your mouth. Move your tongue away from the roof of your mouth and consider any tastes that you are aware of.

5. Take your thumb to your index finger. Slide the pad of your thumb across the prints of this finger and then your other fingers, noticing the sensitive nature of each fingertip as you do.

6. Hold every sense in your awareness.

MEDITATE
TO THE BEAT

If you are not used to slowing down, listening with your senses can seem to be a difficult task. But you can help yourself along by focusing on something consistent—like music—that will hold your attention. Find a type of music that is particularly relaxing for you, and only use it for your meditation practice so that over time you will associate these beats with your feelings of relaxation in meditation.

First, you'll need to build a relaxation playlist for yourself. This could be a favorite song list or a relaxing instrumental piece, or you could search for binaural beats, which are melodies set to certain frequencies that might generate meditative or relaxing effects in you. You don't want to be too distracted by the lyrics or the content of the music itself, but if you're really struggling to settle, you could try singing or dancing along to one favorite song first to expend some energy, before moving on to a playlist that won't be too distracting. Once you have your playlist, use it during your meditation like this:

1. Focus your mind on the music to begin your meditation. Feel the rhythm of the sound waves within your body.
2. Listen to your playlist with and without headphones, noting how the sound changes and sensing any differences in the beats in each ear.
3. Bring your attention back to the music if you find yourself getting distracted by your thoughts throughout your meditation.

INVITE IN THE
SMALL SOUNDS

In what can be a noisy world, your brain is an amazing filter that helps you differentiate the signals from the static. But external sound can become a barrier to your own internal world. You might fill silence with chatter, always use headphones when you leave the house, or fall asleep with the TV on in the background, all to avoid being alone in the quiet with your thoughts. Resist the urge to fill every silence. Practice peaceful solitude by deciding what inputs you'll pay attention to, and be still in the serenity.

1. Listen for the sounds around you where you sit.
2. Sort through the various sounds, and identify the farthest unique sound you can hear. This might be outside the place you are sitting. Consider the fact that silence is never going to be the absence of all noise. Rather, this exercise is about hearing the small things that are always present but so often drowned out, such as a bird chirping or the wind rustling leaves.
3. Tune in to the sounds within the place where you sit, noticing how these are different and distinct to the noises outside.
4. Take your awareness to the sounds closest to you, listening to your breath as you inhale and exhale.
5. Receive all sounds from both near and far into your awareness, like one woven tapestry.

TAP IN TO TOUCH
FOR FOCUSED ATTENTION

It can be difficult to maintain focus when your mind is full of worried thoughts that are begging for your attention. Matching your focus with a very subtle sense of touch can help calm an anxious mind. This form of meditation is often done with a beaded necklace held between the thumb and fingers, and every time a mantra is repeated you count one bead. But it can also be done with your fingers to add another tactile experience to your meditation, which can help keep you focused.

1. Rest your hands with your palms facing up.
2. Curl your fingers in slightly, and on your right hand, touch your thumb to your index finger.
3. Bring your awareness to a focal point. This could be a mantra, a phrase, or a sensation like your breath.
4. Every time you complete one repetition of your chosen focal point—saying your mantra to yourself or completing a breath, for instance—slide your thumb to the next finger. Notice the sensation on the pads of your fingers as you do so.
5. When you reach your littlest finger, continue the process by moving your thumb back along each finger back toward your index finger.
6. When you've returned to your index finger, mark one completed round by tucking in one finger on your left hand.
7. Repeat your rounds on your right hand until you have counted five rounds on your left hand.

DISCOVER
YOUR SIXTH SENSE

You actually have more than five senses. An important sense for meditation—and one that can be strengthened through practice—is a sense of what is going on inside your body. This ability, called interoception, is about feeling the subtle sensory messages within you, such as how your stomach grumbles and pangs when you're hungry or how your chest tightens when you're experiencing anxiety. You could be used to avoiding, overcompensating, or otherwise disconnecting from these sensations. Take time to listen to and receive these messages from your body to develop greater insight into what you feel, both in meditation and in your daily experiences. Here's how:

1. Scan your body starting at your feet.
2. Observe any sensations that you feel, such as tingling, pulsing, tightness, compression, numbness, cold, or warmth.
3. Travel slowly with your awareness to other areas of your body, investigating each one as you move up through your legs, seat, torso, arms, hands, neck, and head.
4. If you find any area of discomfort, pause to investigate it. Consider what it would be like to tolerate that feeling for a while. Shift your position and see how the sensation changes.
5. Explore the sensations of your body with curiosity, building a feeling that you understand your body and what it is telling you it requires—and that you can tolerate or respond to what you need to.

TOUCH AND
SENSE INTERNALLY

Touch is such a powerful and sensitive sense. Combining touch with movement is a great way to build your sense of interoception. In this meditation, you'll notice how your body moves under your touch and compare how you feel in your body when you move one side and then the other. It's subtle and requires slowing down and listening. If you're anxious and stressed, taking this time for yourself to build body awareness and enhance your mind-body connection can be beneficial.

1. Place your left hand on your right collarbone.
2. Raise your right arm up to the ceiling. As you do so, notice how your collarbone moves and how this area shifts below your hand. It might be very subtle in your body.
3. Begin to move your right arm in circles. This could be in a windmill motion, moving your arm in a clockwise motion down to your side and raising it back up, or it could be as if you're drawing circles on the ceiling with your arm staying high in the air. It doesn't matter what it looks like—simply move intuitively in your shoulder and, as you do, again notice how your collarbone shifts, moves, and changes and what this feels like.
4. Continue with this movement for five full breaths.
5. Rest your arms. Detect any difference, no matter how small, in how your right shoulder feels compared with your left shoulder.
6. Repeat on the other side.

LISTEN
TO NATURE

As meditation is an inward-looking practice, a source of anxiety for you could be that you are too focused on yourself. Meditation is about looking within, but this doesn't mean being self-centered, self-important, or self-aggrandizing. These tendencies are rooted in ego, whereas meditative practice is about becoming less attached to these ideas about yourself and more connected to everything. Counter negative and egotistical anxieties with this reminder that you're part of something bigger. Follow these steps:

1. Find a place you can access that is in nature, away from city noise, traffic, and busyness. You might not be able to fully get away from these noises, but even in a city park away from the road, these sounds will fade into the distance.
2. Take a slow walk and focus your attention on the sounds that you hear.
3. Identify an individual noise and follow it when it takes your awareness. Perhaps it's an insect buzzing, a breeze rustling branches, or your footsteps crunching sticks and leaves on the path beneath your feet.
4. Whenever a new sound emerges, spend some time following it, noticing its quality as it moves toward or away from you.
5. Acknowledge the sounds of beauty around you that you might otherwise not hear when you are more focused on your day-to-day life and your inner experiences. Meditate on your connection to these sounds in nature as a listener and a witness.

SEE YOURSELF
CLEARLY WITH LOVE

When was the last time you *really* looked at yourself? Many people avoid consciously looking at themselves. And when they do take a look, it's often with judgment. This dissatisfaction can reflect not only your beliefs about your appearance, but also your broader relationship with yourself. Try this gazing meditation with a mirror to take the time to really see yourself with openness and curiosity.

1. Look at your face in a mirror.
2. Notice how you feel when looking at yourself. Put a name to the specific feelings that arise, and pay attention to whether they are of aversion and a negative nature or whether they are accepting, loving, and positive.
3. Check in with the physical areas where any negative feeling might be showing up—for example, in a clenched jaw, furrowed brow, or pained expression.
4. Allow whatever you feel to arise without trying to push it away or judge it.
5. Hold your own gaze for several minutes. Let this be gentle and rested, not fixated and staring.
6. Note as many small details as you can about your eyes—your irises, pupils, eyelashes, etc. Notice how what you see changes over the minutes (if it does).
7. Relax any physical points of tension you identified. Smile softly to yourself and see how this changes your eyes.
8. Find beauty in these smallest of details. Hold your gaze with love.

SAVOR THE SATISFACTION OF TASTE

Taste is a sense that can offer immense pleasure. But if you're stressed or feeling anxious—and especially if you have a difficult relationship with what you eat and what you allow yourself to put in your body—you might forget the joy that comes with savoring food. Perhaps you feel guilty for having a snack. Maybe you skip breakfast altogether, eat your lunch at your desk while still working, or consume dinner while distracted by media feeds. Take the opportunity for a break at mealtimes, and come back to a sense of delight in the food you eat. Here's how:

1. Commit to eating a meal mindfully. Turn off any TV shows, music, or artificial noises around you that you can control.
2. Look at your food and take in the colors, textures, and variety on your plate. Pay attention to the small details, like steam drifting gently into the air.
3. Notice any smells you can take in.
4. Observe any anticipation in your body, such as salivation in your mouth.
5. Take a bite, paying full attention to every flavor you can sense and noticing how what you smell changes throughout the experience and contributes to what you taste.
6. Focus only on the sensations of eating throughout your meal. If thoughts emerge about your to-do list or about other things causing you anxiety, come back to the present moment and this experience of taste.

REMEMBER THE SCENT
OF RELAXATION

Your sense of smell is highly connected to your memories. It's why a certain food, perfume, or other distinct aroma has the power to transport you back to the time and place that you associate with that scent. Try meditating with a soft, pleasant scent from incense or aromatic candles to create an association for yourself between a specific fragrance and a relaxed state of being. As you begin to associate the scent with this feeling, you can more quickly get into a meditative state.

1. Light a stick of incense or a scented candle. You might close your eyes for this meditation to focus on smell only and heighten this sense, or you might keep your eyes open and watch the smoke or flame with a rested gaze.
2. Inhale through your nose, paying attention to every detail of the scent.
3. Exhale through your nose, noticing the change in what you smell as you do. Your awareness of the intensity of the smell could be less as you breathe out from your lungs and more as you take breath in from your environment.
4. As you breathe in and notice the greater intensity of the scent, inhale a feeling of relaxation.
5. As you breathe out and notice the diminished intensity of the scent, exhale any stress you feel.
6. Continue in this way, inhaling relaxation and exhaling any feelings of stress or anxiety whenever your mind becomes caught up in thought.

MASSAGE
AWAY TENSION

Touch can be incredibly healing. Even simply holding hands with someone can enhance the rest-and-digest response and lower feelings of stress and anxiety. You can also tap in to the power of touch on yourself. If you store a lot of physical tension in your jaw, between your eyebrows, or generally in your face, this little massage can help you to soften and unwind.

1. Identify any areas of tension you are holding in your face.
2. Take your earlobes between your thumb and index finger, and gently pull your fingers down your ears with a small squeeze. Repeat five times.
3. Gently place your index finger and middle finger in front of the top of your ears on each side of your face. With a soft press, draw a line down your jaw to your chin. Play around with feeling where you get a nice massage by adjusting your finger placement up and down slightly on your jaw, or by opening your mouth as you do this. Repeat five times.
4. With the same two fingers, find the space between your eyebrows. Softly pressing your fingertips into your face, trace a slight upward arch over your brows to your temples, and gently rub several small circles with your fingers on your temples. Repeat five times, making a higher arch over your forehead each time.
5. Notice again any tension you are holding in your face and how you feel now.

MASTER ANY INTERRUPTION

When you're in an environment or situation that you can't control, it can be stressful. You could be trying to read a book on a train and be distracted by a crying baby three seats back, or maybe physical sensations distract you from being able to be present in your meditation. As you work on training your attention to different senses and becoming more grounded in present awareness, you might begin to gain greater control of the information that you take in from your senses and the ways you process these disturbances.

Next time you're becoming worked up about a distraction in a situation where you can't directly control the interruption, follow these steps:

1. Pause what you're doing.
2. Close your eyes.
3. Scan your senses one at a time to become aware of everything in your environment. What can you hear, both near you and far off? What can you smell? Taste? Notice any points of touch and contact between your body and where you are.
4. Take everything you can sense into your awareness. Don't let any one sense—or any element of an individual sense, such as a particular sound—have more importance than another. Zoom out to the full experience of your environment in the present moment.
5. Blink your eyes open to return to the space, no longer solely fixated on the one thing that was vying for your attention.

CHAPTER 7

MEDITATIONS TO CHALLENGE YOUR THINKING PATTERNS

How you think can be a habit or pattern that you repeat. If what you play in your mind is a distorted loop of negativity, it will worsen your stress and anxiety. The next few chapters will help you identify your thinking patterns, dismantle unhelpful habits, and constructively establish positive qualities that can enhance your well-being. Changing your mind is not a fast or easy process. This chapter will help you to see your thoughts for what they are and to work toward more realistic and helpful ways of thinking that better manage your stress and anxiety in the long term.

SEE WHAT *IS* WITHOUT OVERTHINKING

Your brain can process thoughts quickly or slowly. Fast thoughts are automatic responses, such as when you turn your head toward a loud noise. Slow thoughts are your logical mind helping you make sense of your experience. Think of these two processes like responses to a smoke alarm. Your fast thinking registers the immediate signal. Your slower thinking identifies whether the house is on fire or something on the stove is smoking. You need both ways of thinking, but there is such a thing as overthinking things, scanning for threats or finding significance where there need not be any. For example, you could build up a story in your mind about the meaning behind someone not texting you back, believing they are upset with you, when they could simply be busy. Use these steps to put a stop to overthinking before you spiral into negative rumination.

1. Stay with any thoughts that arise in your meditation that involve situations causing you anxiety.
2. Ask yourself the following questions about the situation: What are the facts? What do I know for sure? How do I know these things are true?
3. Identify any stories within your thoughts that include details other than these facts. Are they unhelpful narratives? Challenge yourself to come up with ten alternative explanations.
4. See the situation realistically, challenge anything unhelpful, and identify any signals that are true that you need to act on.

DON'T SUFFER TWICE; TAKE A NEW PERSPECTIVE

The Stoic philosophers thought that it's not so much what happens to you that upsets you, but how you perceive the things that happen to you. Two people can experience the same thing and have very different perspectives on it. Losing a job can be a relief to someone who views it as an opportunity to move on, or it can be a devastating stress to someone who sees only the loss. Come to this meditation when you need to see something in a new way. Note that this isn't about denying negative experiences and papering over them with false positivity. This is about processing the experience in a realistic yet useful way to move forward.

1. Pay attention to any thoughts that come up in this meditation that center on difficulties you have faced or are facing.
2. Pinpoint any negative judgments, feelings, or perceptions in the way that your thoughts are shaped around this situation. For example, name any worry, fear, self-pity, or hopelessness.
3. Find a way to reframe the thought as an opportunity. For example, change "I have to start over" to "I get to start over."
4. Practice flipping this perspective from disaster to opportunity so that you don't add additional mental suffering to the difficulties you need to face.

EMBRACE
THE GRAYS

Your brain likes to sort things into easily understandable categories. Yet life is often messy. Few things are all good or all bad, or easily sorted into distinct boxes. It's tempting to reach for black-and-white thinking as a defense tactic from the discomfort this fact produces. You can swing from two extreme poles—for example, thinking you're either awesome or a failure, rather than someone with strengths and weaknesses who experiences highs and lows. This kind of all-or-nothing thinking is often unproductive, as it limits your beliefs and keeps you stuck. Use this meditation to put things into a healthier, more honest perspective by embracing the beauty that can be found in the grays.

1. During meditation, follow any thoughts that arise where you feel things about yourself, a situation, or a problem will never change. Watch out for ideas like "It's either one thing or nothing," "It will always be like this," or "My life will never get any better."
2. Identify the extremes that form the way you're thinking.
3. Think of ten alternative ways of seeing these thoughts. Be creative. Consider the opportunities within each pole. See a spectrum of possibilities. Recall times where these extremes were not true. Let your mind entertain any idea that comes to mind, no matter how seemingly impossible. Approach this exercise with humility and childlike curiosity, knowing that you don't know everything and that the possibilities are endless.

LEAVE THE
PAST BEHIND

Stress is designed to be felt in the present to urge you into action, but broader anxieties can cause you to ruminate on the past. You might dwell on something you said or did that you regret, or something you wish you could change but can't. You might idealize the past as being better than the present, or you might feel things have been unfair. This kind of thinking causes difficult-to-resolve stress that robs you of joy in the present. Don't let past things that can't be changed ruin your present too. Let go with this meditation in order to live in the here and now.

1. Identify if your thoughts during meditation are replaying something from the past that has already happened.
2. Reflect on any feelings that accompany this situation. Pay particular attention to any sense of helplessness around something you can't change, any feeling of unfairness coming from your ego and your expectations, as well as any wistfulness for an imagined ideal.
3. Ask yourself the following questions about this memory: Can I control or influence this situation or its impacts now? Ten minutes from now, will this matter? Will it matter in ten days? Ten months? Ten years?
4. As you consider time lines further into the future, notice whether your feelings about this event and its significance shift or change at all. Set a resolution to be fully present and alive, here and now.

LET THE FUTURE UNFURL ITSELF

The fact that your brain can anticipate things that haven't happened yet is an amazing cognitive development. Thinking about the future can help you to minimize risks and work toward larger goals. At the same time, this ability could make you stressed and miserable if you're always working to control what might happen, assuming things will turn out badly, or wishing for something up ahead in a way that takes you out of the present. Stop fixating on the future. Trust the process and let the story unfold.

1. As thoughts arise in your meditation, notice any that are obsessed with things that haven't happened yet. Identify, in particular, any worries about things going wrong or thoughts about things you don't yet have that you feel you need in order to be happy.

2. Scan for any feelings associated with these future-fixated thoughts. Notice the ways in which apprehension, unhappiness, or other negative emotions could be visiting you in relation to things that haven't even happened yet.

3. Put this future fear or future grasping into context. Recall a time in the past where the future didn't turn out as you had predicted or as you'd hoped. Consider how worrying about future loss steals your peace in the present. Think about how grasping for what you don't have prevents you from being content now.

4. Meditate on the fact that you don't know what's going to happen with an excitement to find out what does.

SEE OPPORTUNITY, NOT CATASTROPHE

If you have a tendency to leap to the worst-case scenario, have you ever stopped to reflect on how often in the past that scenario actually played out as you had feared? Thinking through all the terrible things that could go wrong might give you a temporary sense of being in control of whatever causes you to worry. But fretting about unlikely events is a waste of energy that prevents you from realistically determining what you should do now. Use this meditation to stop catastrophizing before it stops you from enjoying the present.

1. Observe any thoughts that come up in your meditation that have you asking "what if?" *What if* something happens or doesn't happen? *What if* things get worse? *What if* things never change?

2. Examine this thought: How likely is this to happen? Assign a probability on a scale of one to five, where five is "definitely going to happen."

3. Anything with a score of less than three is "unlikely to happen." Let go of the energy spent on concerns of three or less.

4. For concerns scoring greater than three, imagine what you will do if these things happen. Prioritize what you can control. Identify one small action you can take now to prevent or mitigate the impact of the outcome you want to avoid. Make a plan to take action if you need to.

5. Refocus from your what-if scenario to what you can actually do now.

TRUST THE PROCESS; RELEASE CONTROL

How in control you feel plays a big part in how stressed and anxious you feel. Even the illusion that you can influence things can help you feel more at ease. So it makes sense that you would try to control things. But there are few things in life under your direct authority, and trying to control what's out of your hands will make you even more anxious. Enhance your well-being with a focus on what's in your power—your beliefs, actions, and will—and let the outcomes take care of themselves.

1. If you find yourself stressed during meditation, check in for thoughts or feelings of being out of control. These could be about a goal, person, environment, or situation that you wish you could dictate.
2. Feel how it is to desire this control to get what you want. How does it show up in your body through anxious feelings?
3. Examine the source of your thoughts. Are you seeing things accurately? Is the perspective you're taking healthy, or could you look at it in a new way?
4. Consider one small next step you could take, and make a plan toward this action.
5. Acknowledge that you don't control the outcome, but you have the will to do what you can. Fall in love with the process and the uncertainty of not knowing what's going to happen. Feel content knowing that you are putting your energy into what's in your control.

DON'T GIVE AWAY YOUR POWER TO JUDGMENT

Whether you judge others, feel judged by them, or are your own worst critic, judgment can be a comfort mechanism for dealing with negative thoughts. A harsh judgment provides distance between you and others, or even you and yourself. It's sometimes a way of appearing not to care, though underneath a judgment is often something about yourself that you fear. For example, judging appearance could signal insecurities about being unworthy. Resenting someone else's success could point to fears of failure in yourself. Judgment is a covering you might wrap yourself up in like a cloak so that your vulnerability isn't exposed, but this also keeps you in the dark. Don't let judgment, whether of yourself or others, hold power over you and block out your light.

1. If a judging thought comes up in meditation, hold it in your mind and consider it. Are you judging yourself or someone else, or ruminating on someone's judgment of you?

2. Whatever it is, investigate it as something within yourself. Where is this judgment coming from? Are you trying to gain the approval or love of others? Or are you distancing yourself from others or a part of yourself that you don't like?

3. See this judgment for what it is. Is it true? Is it helpful?

4. Let these observations open you up rather than close you off. What would happen if you stopped this judgment? How would you feel?

5. Replace judgment with empathy.

COMPARE YOURSELF ONLY TO YOURSELF

Theodore Roosevelt famously said that "comparison is the thief of joy." When you compare yourself to others, you create an unrealistic picture that inevitably causes stress and anxiety because it is unattainable. It isn't real. You contrast a detailed inner knowledge of your own complicated reality with the incomplete, simple portrait someone else presents. You can't know how they struggle or what they go through when you see only their highlight reel. And rather than inspiring you toward your goals, comparison is rarely motivating. It makes you feel "not good enough." Release the anxiety of comparison and reclaim your joy by focusing on how you meet your own standards.

1. Notice any thoughts that arise in meditation that dwell on comparison. Pay particular attention to any feelings of envy or unfairness that you experience.
2. Consider the standards you are using to assess yourself in the thoughts that arise. Are these your own or someone else's ideas?
3. Make a commitment to yourself to meet your own standards and to let go of those that come from the expectations of others. Compare yourself only to your own self from the day before.
4. Notice the feelings you paid attention to in meditation as they come up in your daily life. Scrolling social media is a big source of comparison! Curate your influences and your thoughts with this reminder that you are on your own journey to your own standards.

DEFEAT
LIMITING BELIEFS

Handling stress and anxiety can be impossible if you believe that there is nothing you can do. The thing is, if you think you can't do something, you'll probably prove yourself right. If you think you can do something, you just might accomplish it. Learned helplessness can take hold if you've spent long enough feeling unable to influence your situation. Responding effectively to stress requires a belief in your abilities and a growth mindset that sees everything as full of potential and possibility. Use this meditation to beat back stress by replacing limiting beliefs with growth beliefs.

1. Catch any thoughts in your meditation that include negative situations you think will never change.
2. Name any emotions that come up as you think about this situation—such as feelings of helplessness, fear, or failure.
3. Identify any limiting words or ideas in your thinking about this situation. Watch out for phrases like "I can't," "I'm not capable enough," or "There's no point in even trying."
4. Flip anything you've identified and view it through a growth mindset. Change any "can't" statement to a "can" statement with whatever needs to be true to make this leap—for example, "I can't do this now—but I *can* learn." Take action; this trumps worrying about those talents or abilities you might think you lack. For things you want that feel impossible for you, add the word *yet* to the statement.

PRACTICE
IMPERFECTION

Perfectionism is paralyzing. It can prevent you from starting or completing something out of a fear that it will never be as good as you want it to be. It can also make you miserable and disappointed, as you set yourself up for expectations that are unattainable. It's impossible to be perfect. Release the weight of striving for perfection from your shoulders by focusing on your efforts and enjoying the journey.

1. If your meditation brings up a situation involving a sense you have that things need to be perfect, pause on it to examine it.
2. Don't worry about the ultimate end goal or outcome; instead, focus on the steps you need to undertake toward a favorable outcome. What process do you need to put in place or go through? What are the actions that you need to take toward the outcome? Think about it like you're a coach. Your goal is to win the game, but instead of just thinking about that outcome, take action on the details needed to play a good game so that the result takes care of itself.
3. Let go of seeing anything less than perfect as a failure. Consider that the effort is enough—that the details will add up to the outcome, even if that outcome is imperfect. Take pride in your efforts. Find joy in the process.

DON'T PLEASE OTHERS; PLEASE YOUR AUTHENTIC SELF

Worrying about how others see you is common—we're social beings, after all. But this worry could lead you to try to please others at the expense of your own authentic self in a bid to be accepted. People-pleasing is part of your ego's concern about how others see you. Over time, you can lose your sense of self due to the constant pressure to perform in a way that goes against your real truth. Use these steps to return to your true self through a commitment to align your values with your thoughts, words, and actions.

1. In your time of meditation, observe any thoughts that arise where you feel a lack of alignment between your true feelings and the things you say or do with others. Search, in particular, for feelings of obligation or pressure to do what someone else wants in order to keep the peace or make them like you.

2. Notice how this makes you feel. Identify any areas of tension this causes within your body.

3. Identify the fears underlying your behavior. Are you worried that this person won't like you or will reject you in some way?

4. Imagine that you acted in line with your truth in the situation or relationship. What would this look like? What would this feel like? What would happen?

5. Commit to be true to your own values going forward, and embody this in your thoughts, words, and actions.

ACCENTUATE
THE POSITIVE

As much as stress and anxiety lead to outright negative feelings, a perhaps less obvious impact is their ability to downplay positive emotions. It's strange to think that you might worry about enjoying something too much, but consider whether there are times you minimize your positive experiences. You might devalue a success or pretend something was unimportant. It's almost as if the fear of happiness leaving makes you not want to feel its full strength in the moment. Don't shy away from experiencing the fullness and richness of life. It's just as important to feel through your good emotions as it is to feel through your difficult ones.

1. Notice any thoughts in your meditation that relate to successes or happy moments, and spend some time considering what emerges.
2. Pay attention to how recalling these memories feels in your body. Are you full of lightness and energy? Or are there places you hold back?
3. Search your thinking about these positive experiences for any ways in which you play down the good. Watch for any "yeah, but..." qualifiers that you append to the good thoughts, where negative ideas compete with fully experiencing positivity.
4. As you inhale, breathe in complete satisfaction and joy.
5. As you exhale, breathe out any heaviness and limitations on your delight.
6. Let yourself relax into this feeling and fully experience the happiness.

CHAPTER 8

MEDITATIONS TO BEFRIEND YOUR EMOTIONS

The emotions that accompany stress, worry, and anxiety can be intense and difficult to handle. As a result, your instinct might be to try to avoid or get rid of any negative feelings. But if you resist what you feel, these emotions will only persist within you. Meditation can help you to feel what you feel in a safe way, allowing you to be a witness and friend to anything painful or hard to handle. This chapter is about learning to recognize, listen to, and understand your emotions so that you can find peace.

NAME AND LOCATE
WHAT YOU FEEL

Emotions come and go like waves. They might be triggered by something obvious, or you might not even know why you suddenly feel a certain way. Think of emotions as information telling you something about what you need or want. However, when you're distressed by anxiety, it can be more difficult to understand these messages. You might not be used to sitting with what you feel and might usually disconnect from, or push away, strong feelings. Use this meditation to start to recognize and label what you feel, which can enable you to master your emotions so they don't master you.

1. Examine any intense feelings that come up during your meditation using the following **RAIN** method.
2. **R**ecognize the emotion. Name it. Specifically acknowledging what you feel lessens the power of the feeling, even if only subtly at first.
3. **A**llow the feeling to be there. This doesn't mean you think it's "good" or "right" or that you like it. But resist the urge to feel you "should" be a certain way. The feeling simply is. Don't try to deny how you feel; this is about experiencing what you feel safely.
4. **I**nvestigate the feeling. Where do you feel this in your body? In your mind?
5. **N**urture what you feel. Know that this feeling is not how you'll always feel. Send love to it. Don't overly identify with the feeling as if it were saying something fundamental about you.

LEARN TO TRUST YOUR FEELINGS

As a social being, it's natural for you to care about the opinions of others. However, if you start to trust others' judgments of what you feel more than you trust your own, this tendency can compound anxiety and be damaging to you. If you've ever been told you shouldn't feel the way you do or had your feelings invalidated, you could come to doubt yourself and might try to find ways to escape from your inner world. Try this meditation when you're insecure in what you feel.

1. Catch any emotions arising in meditation that you usually dismiss with the thought that you shouldn't feel that way. Name the feeling.
2. Give permission to the feeling to stay this time. Remember that experiencing it doesn't mean you need to act on it.
3. Scan your body for where this feeling shows up in any physical sensations. Are you holding yourself anywhere or tensing against something?
4. Counter any doubts about this feeling by holding it with security. Let go of any emotional, physical, or mental energy you usually spend masking this emotion.
5. Ask yourself—now that you are no longer thinking things should be anything different and now that you are holding this feeling with security—what is this feeling asking for? Take responsibility for your emotions. Plan to have a conversation about what's bothering you if you need to, or simply spend time letting the feeling move through you.

LEARN TO SIT
WITH THE PANIC

If you've struggled with anxiety for a long time, you could experience a lot of panic when facing your emotions. The masking strategies you use can help numb you against really difficult feelings, but they also diminish the good stuff. Balance is needed between these two extremes so that you can truly feel what's real without judgment. Practice this meditation when you're feeling safe so that it can translate to a feeling of capability when you need it most: when any panic arises.

1. As you watch your thoughts in meditation, strong feelings that you have been suppressing as you go about the busyness of your daily life could surface. Name whatever comes up.
2. Know that you're safe to let this feeling express itself fully.
3. Notice how your body moves or feels as you sit with this emotion. Remember that you're safe where you sit and that you can tolerate this while you examine it. What is your body asking you to feel? Let it happen, and even exaggerate the effect. You might hunch your shoulders in, shake your limbs and hands, or curl inward on yourself.
4. Be still, and send a feeling of safety to the places where you feel the anxiety rising. Try taking one of your hands and placing it on the areas of your body where the emotion is strongest, such as your chest or shoulder. Feel this kind gesture calm any panic with safety.

DEVELOP LOVING-KINDNESS WHEN YOU'RE ANGRY

Few emotions have the power to control you like anger does. If you try to resist this pull and "fix" it rather than feel it, your efforts can have the opposite effect: The hate and bitterness you feel embeds even further in your resistance and defensiveness. Trying to be calm and controlled when you feel anything but can contribute even more stress. It's okay to get upset at times. Emotions need to be experienced. The key is to develop the skills to allow emotions to move through you to a point where they're not so large. An excellent way to do this when you're angry is to practice loving-kindness.

1. Notice the nature and shape of the anger you feel and how this manifests in your mind and body.
2. Repeat the mantra for this meditation: "May you be happy. May you be healthy. May you be peaceful."
3. Think of yourself and send yourself this wish.
4. Think of someone you love in your life and send them this wish.
5. Think of a friend you like and send them this wish.
6. Think of an acquaintance you don't know that well and send them this wish.
7. Think of someone who challenges you and send them this wish.
8. Think of yourself as connected to everyone and everything in an ever-widening, fully embracing circle. Send this wish to all.

ENCIRCLE
ANY SHAME

Shame is a strong emotion that you might not often consciously think about, but if you look for it, you might find it lurking underneath many negative emotions. It's a feeling of not being okay as you are. Emotions themselves are not good or bad. Just because it feels bad doesn't mean it is bad. It's the judgment of something as good and bad that leads to deep feelings of unworthiness. Try this meditation to get to the root of any shame that you feel.

1. Name any strong emotions that cause you to feel unworthy or like you're not okay in some way.
2. Picture yourself as a child. You might initially think this feels silly, but stick with it.
3. Ask the following: What does this child need when they are upset? What does this child need when they feel bad and not okay?
4. Bring these unconscious needs you identified up to the conscious level. See the child as they are, and hold them (exactly as they are) with understanding and unconditional love.
5. Wrap your arms around the child in a big hug. Tell the child they are okay and that they are worthy as they are, even the parts they think are bad.
6. Take this feeling of protectiveness for the child and zoom it outward to yourself as you are now, wrapping any feelings of shame within you with love.

TURN WORRY
TO WONDER

So often it is fear that underpins stress and anxiety. Fear of what you can't control. Fear of what you can't change or of what's going to happen. Fear of yourself or others. This emotion is part of your nervous system's response to threats, enabling you to constantly adapt and take action. But when you're in a state of chronic anxiety, it can also deplete enormous amounts of energy and inhibit your complex and rational thinking skills. So, as you get used to naming what you feel and letting it move through you, it's also important to build skills to respond to those emotions you find that are not helping you or are causing you harm. Come to this meditation to start transforming your relationship with your fears.

1. When you experience anxious feelings in meditation, go deeper. What fear lies underneath the feeling?
2. Approach this fear with curiosity. Notice if your mind is on the present, the past, or the future. Find any points where you're exaggerating or imagining things that contribute to the fear.
3. Scan your body for any sensations that come up with this emotional experience.
4. Flip your worry into wonder by separating the feeling (fear) from your thoughts about it ("this is scary"). When the emotion isn't the same as how you think about it, you're free to tell a new story ("this is exciting"). Choose possibility over limitation. Choose excitement over fear. Choose wonder over worry.

LAUGH WHEN THINGS ARE OVERWHELMING

Modern life is, in a word, *busy*. Trying to balance family, friends, work, and health can be overwhelming, and you might feel like something always suffers as you try to take care of all of your priorities at once. When you feel like you can't do everything, you might freeze, shut down, and do nothing instead. You might get even further behind as a result, compounding your stress and anxiety. It sounds strange, but laughing can help. Laughter reduces the strength of the negative emotions you feel and can help you feel in control. Try this funny little meditation as a release when you feel overwhelmed.

1. Tune in to your breath as you breathe in and out from your nose.
2. Yawn, stretching your jaw as big as you comfortably can as you inhale through your mouth.
3. Close your mouth with a yawning exhale and smile softly to yourself. Begin to grin, smiling with your teeth so that the smile reaches your eyes.
4. Start to laugh to yourself. It can feel weird to laugh without a joke or other trigger. It might feel fake or forced. But, still, laugh.
5. Engage your whole body as you laugh harder and harder, shaking through your chest and shoulders and feeling a laugh deep from within your belly.
6. Stop laughing when you've had enough, and come back to stillness. Notice the silence around you and take stock of how you feel now.

BE A FRIEND WHEN YOU FEEL LONELY

Some people react to stress and anxiety by isolating themselves. Sadly, loneliness can make anxiety even worse. It distorts your thinking, making you believe you don't matter and no one cares. Withdrawing might make you feel like you can inoculate yourself against disappointment and rejection. Perhaps you find it difficult to ask for help and don't want to be a burden. It can feel scary and vulnerable to open up to others. But this vulnerability isn't a weakness—it's the path to deeper self-awareness and deeper connections to others. If you feel lonely, consider this meditation to help you reconnect.

1. Notice any feelings of loneliness that arise and put a label to them.
2. Rather than push away the feelings, let them be here. Observe how these feelings make your body feel.
3. Think of someone in your life that you can reach out to. You don't need to ask for anything for yourself; when you need a friend, you can *be* a friend to someone and you'll create the same benefits of connection.
4. Make a plan to ask this person for a coffee, a walk, a chat, or some company in the next week.
5. Hold that person in your mind and send a wish of loving-kindness to them that they may feel loved, accepted, and connected.
6. Send this wish to yourself. Remember that although there is a vulnerability in connection, it's through this risk that love and acceptance come.

GAIN PERSPECTIVE WHEN UPSET WITH SOMEONE

Your brain is a storytelling machine. Stories about yourself, others, and the world around you help you make sense of things. But the story you tell and the way things are in reality are not necessarily a perfect relationship. If your narrative shortcuts are always negative, especially when it comes to others, they might be unhelpful stories to tell yourself. If you're upset with someone, try this meditation to write a new story.

1. If you find yourself ruminating in your meditation on someone you're upset with, focus on the situation.
2. Consider the story you're telling yourself. Are you in control or out of control? Do you think their behavior is to do with you or is it on them? Is the story true? Is it useful or helpful to you in addressing things?
3. Notice how you feel in your body. Are you heavy or light? When you are with this person, how do you feel? After you have just spent time with them, how do you feel? Is your energy filled up or drained?
4. Frame how you feel so that you can effectively communicate why you are upset with that person. For example, formulate statements like "I feel…," "I worry that…," or "I need…"
5. Make a plan in your mind about how you'll communicate this to this person or what you want to do about the situation. When talking to them, listen to how they respond and how they feel too.

CARVE OUT
YOUR SORROWS

Kahlil Gibran wrote that "the deeper that sorrow carves into your being, the more joy you can contain." It's not always easy to see this when you're hurting, but you have a choice in the meaning you draw from your negative experiences. In fact, what you value the most is likely to have come out of stress and struggle. What you needed to fight for and how you grew when things were falling apart are what make you. It won't take the sting away from the hurt—you still need to process any pain. But let this meditation be a reminder when you're hurting that the best is yet to come.

1. Gather some paper and a pen for this exercise when painful emotions are too much for a still meditation.
2. Write down the story of what has happened to trigger the emotion.
3. Next, notice whether you have included any feelings in the way you wrote this story or whether it is a more fact-driven account.
4. Focus on the feelings. Write in depth about how you feel. It can be difficult to do this. It's sometimes easier to talk about the details of something that has happened, as it can feel painful to focus on the emotions. Consider that often there is an emotional peak before you widen out to a greater awareness of the meaning of the situation.
5. Release your hurt onto the page.

GO WITH THE FLOW OF UNHAPPINESS

It's natural to want to always be happy in life. But unhappiness is just another emotion that can be fleeting. Think of this emotion as simply information. Perhaps your unhappiness is a call to action to change something in your life. Or perhaps it's something you need to sit with to adjust your expectations and find satisfaction in the present. After all, research suggests that how happy you feel relates more to your expectations than to your objective situation. Investigate your unhappy feelings with this reflection.

1. Pay attention to any feelings of unhappiness that arise in your meditation. Call it what it is in your mind.
2. Resist the urge to push away or judge this feeling. Allow it to be here.
3. Check in with your body and how this feeling shows up. Notice any places of heaviness or tightness.
4. Investigate the source of your unhappiness. Are you seeking happiness in someplace else, in something else, or in someone else? Are you actually more comfortable in your unhappiness? Are your expectations setting you up for unhappiness? Are you taking responsibility here and now for your own happiness?
5. Create an anchor in your values. Even if things aren't as you'd like them to be now, can you find satisfaction in setting your expectations to live with those values that are most important to you?
6. As you probe these questions, notice the quality of how you feel. Notice its edges and subtle flows.

PICK A PATH
THROUGH INDECISION

When you're anxious and stressed out, you don't make the best decisions. Your energy is spent on fighting fires rather than on rational thinking and deliberate action. But indecision costs you. When you face a difficult decision, remember the story of the donkey. Unable to decide between water on one side and hay on the other, the poor animal collapsed before it could choose. Use your emotions as guides to avoid this decision paralysis. While you don't need to act on every feeling, don't view your emotional life as standing in opposition to your rational one either. Emotions are crucial to the process of figuring things out. Try this meditation to see things clearly when you feel indecisive.

1. Catch when your thoughts are fixating on a decision point. It might be a life decision or something small.
2. Before you try to weigh up the logical options in your mind, notice how you feel. How does each option show up in your body when you spend time considering it?
3. Consider what these emotions are communicating. Perhaps you feel anxious, threatened, or excited. Maybe the stakes feel high. What do these emotions really tell you? If you're still not sure, try the game of tossing a coin and noticing how you feel when it lands on a particular option.
4. Trust your gut, and let your feelings point you in the right direction.

ATTEND AND
BEFRIEND THREATS

The ways you respond to anxiety aren't necessarily wrong, but they can be unhelpful. If you have anxiety or have had to adapt in difficult environments in the past, you might have ways of coping that are not appropriate for your life now. This exercise is great to use when you feel threatened so that you can decide on a suitable response.

1. Recognize any feelings of anxiety that arise in your meditation.
2. Allow them to be felt, but as you do, notice any ways in which you would usually respond to protect or distance yourself from them. These could be avoidance, isolation, hypervigilance, compliance, self-pity, hostility, and so on.
3. Whatever you notice, label the feeling or impulse behind it.
4. Observe the label you've created, and notice if you identify with the thought. This might show up, for example, as an "I am…" or "I want to…" statement.
5. Ask what the thought is protecting you from and what it is also blocking from you.
6. Relabel this protection device so that it is a visitor to you, rather than part of your identity. For example, you might say "Right now I feel…" or "Part of me wants to…"
7. Adopt an attend-and-befriend approach to the feeling. Understand your vulnerabilities and the reasons why you take the coping strategy that you do. Identify what isn't serving you so that you can let it go.

CHAPTER 9

MEDITATIONS TO COUNTER FEAR WITH SELF-LOVE

Recognizing and challenging negative patterns that hold you back is vital, but meditating to fill up on the positive is just as important. If you only focus on one aspect, it's a bit like going to the gym while still eating junk food all day. The meditations in this chapter focus on increasing your skills in accessing confidence-boosting beliefs through things like acceptance, compassion, and trust. Dealing with stress and anxiety might make you see yourself in a certain way that isn't necessarily helpful. Try the affirmations in this chapter when you're ready to flip the script and build resiliency.

KNOW YOURSELF THROUGH SELF-AWARENESS

The foundation of any self-inquiry is self-awareness. You might think you know yourself quite well, but the truth is that much of your day is likely based on habits you haven't questioned in a long time. Your thinking is also subject to biases, which means you pay more attention to things that confirm what you already think you know to be true. Come to this meditation with a beginner's mind to cultivate greater self-awareness.

1. Meditate on this affirmation: "I know myself."
2. When your mind wanders in meditation, notice what you're feeling. Acknowledge it; name it; remember that it's only by finding a way to be with your feelings that you can be in tune with who you really are and open yourself to love and to change.
3. Come back to your affirmation once you have recognized the feeling.
4. At the end of your meditation, think about a daily routine of yours. Perhaps you go to the same place for coffee every day or eat the same breakfast or take the same route to and from work. Ask yourself if this is a habit or a genuine preference. Question your assumptions. Challenge yourself to try one new thing in relation to this habit. Take a new route home. Try a new food. Go somewhere new. Shake up your routine and see how you feel.

BEGIN WITH PROFOUND SELF-ACCEPTANCE

If you don't accept something that is part of you, you'll find yourself wasting your energy trying to cover it up, hide it, or change it. This is not only stressful but also futile, because this resistance only pushes things to take deeper root within you. It doesn't go away; it simply feels unseen and rejected. It's vital for your well-being to accept what is part of you at a deep level. This doesn't mean you necessarily have to like it or never change it, but sometimes you need to get closer in order to be able to love it or let it go.

1. Concentrate on this mantra: "I accept." You can add something specific that you are working to accept, or you can keep it simple. Perhaps think of something you would change about yourself if you had a magic wand.
2. Notice how focusing on this mantra feels. Sense whether any resistance or covering strategies are trying to take over.
3. Consider how you think about this part of you that you wish to be different. Do you feel you need it to be "fixed" for you to be okay?
4. For any resistance or desire to fix, try a new perspective. Rather than think you won't be okay until it is different or fixed, realize that it won't be different or fixed until you are okay. Send loving acceptance to what bothers you.

PUT YOURSELF FIRST
WITH SELF–RESPECT

Connection with others is vital to flourishing in life, but that's not to say that it's easy! Conflict can arise and be a point of stress. On the one hand, connection requires openness and vulnerability. But on the other hand, it's important to know yourself and your boundaries—and to be able to assert those boundaries when you need to. Think of a boundary as what you're willing to accept in how others treat you. This isn't about putting unnecessary barriers up, but it is about respecting yourself so that you are in alignment with what you believe in and need.

1. Concentrate on this phrase in your meditation: "I respect myself."
2. Think about a situation where you allowed a boundary to be crossed. This could be a time when you said yes when you meant no, or vice versa, or perhaps a time when you agreed with something you didn't believe in.
3. Notice the way recalling this memory makes you feel and any sensations that show up in your body. Watch out especially for feelings of discomfort, guilt, or fear. These feelings are guides that can tell you a boundary has been crossed. Were you worried about causing problems, losing the relationship, causing a confrontation, or not being liked?
4. Imagine what action you could take next time around to express how you feel and reassert your boundary.
5. Return your thoughts to your meditative phrase.

BELIEVE IN YOURSELF WITH STRONG SELF-ESTEEM

Low self-esteem can be associated with increased stress and anxiety. But self-esteem is a double-edged sword. You need confidence in yourself and your abilities, but if this is not grounded in reality, it can lead to a false sense of grandeur or self-importance that needs constant attention to keep fed. Think of this mental exercise as less about self-belief for self-belief's sake and more about taking action that builds a belief in yourself.

1. Focus on this mantra: "I take action."
2. Think of a situation that is causing you anxiety—where you feel like you're out of your depth.
3. Assess your self-talk. Is it realistic? Consider where your "edge" is in what you're trying to do. Your edge is the point at which you're still learning and growing. It's the point at which things are not so difficult that you set yourself up for failure and not so easy that you're bored and unchallenged.
4. Identify one small next step you can take. You don't have to have a full plan or know where you're going, but an initial planned action is one of the best things you can have to feel more in control and reduce any stress that you feel, resulting in greater self-esteem.

LISTEN TO
YOUR GUT

Being authentic and true to yourself requires a great deal of self-trust. If you're not certain what you feel or what you think, it could make it more difficult to respond to stresses. This might happen because you've been through tough situations when people in your life challenged how you felt or questioned it, causing you now to question yourself and the deep integral messages you are receiving via your emotions and body. Counter self-doubt with trust in what you believe and value.

1. Affirm to yourself, "I trust myself."
2. Recall a time when you weren't sure of yourself. What was your gut saying to you? What did you do? How did it turn out? Would you do anything differently if you could?
3. Pay attention to any feelings of doubt or anxiety that come up with this memory, and notice where these manifest in your body.
4. Think of someone in your life whom you trust. Imagine that person is with you, putting their hand on your shoulder or holding your hand, sending you an energy of trust for any part of you that you doubt.
5. Take your hand and place it on your belly. Your gut can be like a second brain. Examine what it's telling you now as you come back to your affirmation of trust in yourself.

STAY CALM WITH
SELF-CONTROL

Do you ever react in the moment in a way that you later regret? Do you wish you could be calmer when you encounter stressful situations? Although it's important not to deny your feelings but to feel through them, it's equally important to be in control of your feelings or else they will control you. Try this exercise to work through intense emotions and stay in control.

1. Meditate on this phrase: "I take responsibility for myself."
2. If an emotion that makes you feel out of control arises during meditation or in your day-to-day life, pause. Examine it, and label what it is—rage, frustration, neediness, etc.
3. Breathe in for a count for four and out for a count of six. Repeat five rounds of breath in this way, which should equate to roughly 1 minute. Notice if the feeling changes during this minute; perhaps it starts to lessen slightly.
4. Place your palms together in front of you and quickly rub them back and forth for 5 seconds. Pull your hands apart about 1 inch and move them slightly toward and away from each other; notice any heat, friction, and energy this generates and expels from one hand to the other. Check in with whether your feelings are losing energy slightly with this motion.
5. Repeat this breath and friction exercise until you notice the strength of the emotion passing through you with every release and dissipation of the sensation between your hands.

REST AND REJUVENATE
WITH SELF-CARE

Your self-development is not a sprint. It's not about how fast you can "fix" what you don't like. Life isn't really a marathon either. Rather than a mapped course toward a finish line, it's more like a messy squiggle of uphills, downhills, curves, turns, dead ends, and periods of backtracking. You need to take care of yourself on this journey. You need rest and downtime, but in a culture that prizes being busy, this can feel like an unproductive and wasteful use of time, causing even more stress and feelings of guilt. Don't burn yourself out. Take time to recharge. Take care of yourself.

1. Focus your meditation on the following mantra: "I care for myself."
2. Think of a time you felt truly cared for by yourself. What was it about this experience that made you feel this way?
3. Relax into this memory, and as you do, feel the areas of your body that also relax and melt into the supports where you sit.
4. Think of the unique conditions that make you feel taken care of. Identify strategies to build them into your routine on a more regular basis.
5. Hold on to the feeling of being cared for throughout your meditation, coming back to your mantra whenever you get caught up in any particular thoughts.

BE KIND WITH
SELF-COMPASSION

When you think about compassion, you might first think about other people. It's sometimes easier to extend compassion to friends and loved ones than to yourself. The forgiveness and allowance you give to others might not flow so easily in your direction. It's okay to hold yourself to a high standard, but when you're *too* hard on yourself, try viewing yourself like your own best friend and see how that changes things. With compassion first for yourself, you can give more to others too. Extend compassion to yourself through this loving forgiveness practice.

1. Begin with this mantra: "I forgive myself."
2. Next, think of someone in your life that you care for who is very close to you.
3. Take one hand over your heart and focus on this wish for them: "May you be happy. May you be loved. May you be free."
4. Take this wish for your chosen person and now think of yourself. Keep your hand on your heart as you say to yourself: "May I be happy. May I be loved. May I be free."
5. As you think of this wish, feel the breath in your body under your hand on your chest. Feel happiness, love, and freedom radiating toward the center of your being.

ENVELOP YOURSELF IN THE LIGHT OF SELF-LOVE

You're flawed. You will always be striving, and you'll never be able to reach a sense of perfection. This is okay! Perfection isn't the goal. You still need to love yourself—your whole self, the positive and the negative. If you have an aversion to parts of yourself, you will always be in a war with your heart. You'll be resisting, activating your fight-or-flight response, and always reacting from survival mode, while guarded against yourself. Loving yourself, flaws and all, doesn't mean you won't have things to work on or change. On the contrary, change starts from accepting what is within you. Allow this meditation to open you to falling in love with your whole self.

1. Affirm to yourself: "I love." Append something specific if you'd like, or keep it simple.
2. Inhale love in toward yourself.
3. Exhale love out toward the world.
4. As any thoughts or feelings arise that grab for your attention, love them. Don't judge them, try to push them away, or let them go. Even in letting go there can be friction and resistance. Simply love them and thank them for stopping by.
5. Visualize the feeling of love for these thoughts as a ball of light held in your heart. Observe it growing within you and radiate this light outward.

DON'T WAIT FOR
SELF-MOTIVATION

Stress and anxiety can cause you to freeze, feeling unable to do anything. Yet if you sit around waiting for motivation to strike, you might never get started on anything at all. The thing is, action leads to motivation, rather than the other way around. Try these tips to start moving and get into a flow with self-motivation.

1. Meditate on this mantra: "I motivate myself by taking action."
2. Think of something that you'd like to do, but that you struggle to motivate yourself to do.
3. Focus on what tasks are needed. Try to make them realistic and manageable.
4. Next, try the Pomodoro Technique: Set a timer for 20 minutes. For 20 minutes, dedicate yourself to taking mindful action on one thing. Perhaps it's researching what you need to do to get started. Perhaps it's practicing a skill or learning something new. Perhaps it's reaching out for help with something.
5. Notice if you'd like to keep going when the timer goes off. You might be surprised to find that you do. The hardest part can be getting started. But 20 minutes is a small amount of time that can help you kick-start your motivation.

REWRITE YOUR STORY
WITH SELF-BELIEF

Your memory and the stories you tell yourself probably feel more accurate than they actually are. This is a very helpful thing to realize, because it turns out that it is less important how true a story is for you than how useful it is for you. This isn't about creating delusions of grandeur for yourself, but it can help you get rid of stories where you dwell on mistakes and anxieties that only hold you back. It's a very empowering thought: that you can choose what story you tell. Try this meditative exercise to replace self-doubt with self-belief.

1. Before beginning your meditation, take out a pen and some paper.
2. Write down five things you believe to be true about yourself. Don't overthink it. They can be positive or negative. What are the first things that come to mind when you think about yourself?
3. For each item, ask yourself this: Is it a helpful belief? Be less concerned in this exercise about what is true—this is about challenging any beliefs about yourself that aren't serving you.
4. For anything that is unhelpful, meditate on it. Can you find a way to challenge the belief with a more useful perspective?
5. Tune in to your breath as you focus on the affirmation: "I believe in myself." Make this more specific to a positive aspect of yourself or your abilities if you'd like.

BE A SUPERHERO WITH SELF-EFFICACY

You will face obstacles in life—that's a fact. How you view these obstacles and approach them is the key. What the actual obstacle is matters less than you'd think. It matters more that you see things clearly, that you accept what you can and can't control, and that you take action. Fostering a sense of self-efficacy—a belief that you are capable—is one of the biggest positive perspective shifts you can bring to confronting the barriers causing stress and anxiety in your life. If you believe you can change and influence things, you will be more likely to do so.

1. Hold in your mind the following mantra: "I believe I can." You can make this more specific to yourself or keep it broad.
2. Think about something you're trying to do in your life—or something you want to do—but where you are facing an obstacle or don't think you can accomplish it.
3. Notice how contemplating this barrier makes you feel.
4. Imagine an alter ego for yourself. Imagine the kind of person you think could do this thing or overcome this obstacle. Give them a name. It's a bit like make-believe. You might feel silly or like a little kid. Go with it!
5. Embody this persona. Pretend you have all their qualities. Resolve to approach your life with the energy and the skills of this alter ego while you tackle this goal.

CHAPTER 10

MEDITATIONS TO FACE YOUR FEARS

Some experiences, such as public speaking or flying, commonly cause stress and anxiety for many people. Meditations and visualizations can help you consider specific anxiety-producing situations from a safe place. Think of it like a training ground for your mind, to build the mental models it needs to know what to expect and to feel prepared to perform in the real-life scenario. You might still feel the fear—but you'll know you can handle it.

CONFIDENTLY DELIVER
A PRESENTATION

Public speaking is a top fear for many people. A spotlight is on you, and the social stakes can seem high. You don't want to embarrass yourself. You could feel judged and anxious about getting things right. Visualizing yourself delivering a successful speech can help to reduce these anxieties so that you can perform better when you need to.

1. Stand tall with your feet hip-width apart. Take your hands to your hips for a moment in a commanding pose, feeling grounded for several breaths, before releasing your arms by your sides.
2. Imagine the location for your presentation in as much detail as you can. Picture your audience.
3. Take note of any anxious feelings coming up as you picture this.
4. See yourself confident and composed, and practice delivering your speech. Experiment with lowering your voice slightly, which can open your airway and help control your breath to keep you calm. Resist any urge to pace or fidget; come back to an awareness of your breath for a pause when you need to.
5. Visualize the positive response from your audience to what you have to say. Check in to see if any anxiety you felt has lessened with the successful delivery of this speech.
6. Try this exercise in front of a mirror or record yourself to further build confidence.

DO SOMETHING ALONE THAT CHALLENGES YOU

When you're alone in a crowd, it can feel like all eyes are on you. You might find this awkward and anxiety-producing. Merely the thought of eating a meal in a restaurant or going to a theater to watch a movie on your own might make your palms sweat. But there's a benefit in practicing intentional solitude. Lean into this challenge to improve how you relate to yourself and to others.

1. Sit tall and shake out your arms and hands to release any nerves you feel.
2. Imagine in specific detail a place you want to go to that is familiar to you. Envision yourself going there alone. Picture where you will sit and what you will do.
3. Note if any feelings of anxiety come up as you visualize this.
4. Focus briefly on the other people in the place. Observe that no one is taking any notice of you. Note if the feelings of anxiety diminish with the realization that people pay less attention to you than you think they do.
5. Relish the feeling of freedom in this autonomy: You are free to go where you want, do what you want, and stay as long as you want with no other expectations or obligations. Let this freeing feeling flood through any remaining anxiety within you.
6. Make a plan to go alone to a place where you feel comfortable.

ROCK AN
IMPORTANT MEETING

Anxiety can really get in the way of things you want to achieve in life. Maybe you don't speak up because you're too in your head. Perhaps you don't share your ideas because you're worried about how they'll be received. It might make you more comfortable in the short term, but in the long term, playing small will hold you back. Try these perspective shifts to feel the fear and do what you need to do anyway.

1. Sit tall with your shoulders back and your chin held high.
2. Visualize yourself sitting this tall in a meeting room. Picture the details, including everyone in the room.
3. Think of one important thing you want to say in this meeting. Notice how you feel and whether you are nervous thinking about what you want to say.
4. Imagine yourself saying what you've prepared. See the positive and receptive reaction of others in the room, who either don't notice any nervousness that you feel or who view it with compassion. Observe whether this realization helps to resolve any nerves you feel.
5. Prepare one thing to say in an upcoming meeting. Resist the urge to overprepare your point—this sends a message to your anxiety that it's right to be so scared. Prepare enough ahead of time to make you feel confident.

CHANGE A
BAD HABIT

It's difficult if you feel that you can never change your bad habits. Not only are you dealing with something that bothers you, but you feel that it could last forever and that the way things are is how they will always be, even if you don't like it. But everything shifts in time. And you can change. The trick is to start with the small things first and build up a habit over time—small drops of water create a mighty ocean.

1. Change your normal meditation seat. You might cross the opposite ankle, try a chair instead of the ground or vice versa, or stretch your legs out in front of you.
2. Think about a negative habit in your life you want to change.
3. Consider how contemplating this change makes you feel. Perhaps you feel hopeless, frustrated, or afraid.
4. Imagine what your life will look like if you stay the same, and then picture what your life will look like if you change what you're doing.
5. Now, in light of what things could look like if you made the change, revisit the feelings you originally identified. Are any negatives lessened? Is there room for more hope?
6. Plan to make one small change toward a goal that you can commit to and track for the next one hundred days. Give it time to take hold as a new habit. Commit to do things differently so that you can get different results.

CONFRONT A LIFE CHANGE WITH COURAGE

Sometimes big changes hit you out of the blue. Suddenly your future might not look like you thought it would. You need to pick up the pieces and rebuild. It's tempting to curl up under the covers and avoid dealing with things that feel bigger than you in this moment, but this approach has a way of building and blowing up further down the line. The only way out is through. Let your feelings pass through you. Process the loss of what you knew so that a fresh chapter can open up before you when you're ready.

1. Counteract any impulses to shrink into yourself as you sit in meditation. Lengthen your spine, raise your chin, and lift through your chest.
2. Visualize a path ahead of you. You don't know yet where it leads.
3. Notice how you feel. Scan your body for related physical sensations, especially any places of resistance or containment.
4. Picture yourself taking steps down the path. With each step forward, leave behind any need to restrain yourself from deep feelings of grief, anger, or pain.
5. Observe whether this permission to feel enables you to release the well of emotions that is within you. Observe how what you feel intensifies and subsides, perhaps subtly at first, as you let the emotions pass through you.
6. If at any point you do feel too overwhelmed by your emotions, ground yourself in your breath.

FLY
WITHOUT FEAR

If conquering your anxieties were as simple as being rational about them, it would be easy. You might logically know that you are more at risk on your drive to the airport than on the flight itself, but this is cold comfort if you are afraid of flying. This thought alone isn't enough to make you feel safe. Your nervous system still kicks into overdrive, and your emotions still run amok. Try this visualization to build emotional resilience during the experience of flying.

1. Sit back in a chair and let yourself feel totally and completely relaxed, sinking completely into its firm and comfortable support.
2. Envision yourself on your trip to the airport. Picture arriving safely, checking in easily, sailing through security, and finding your gate with plenty of time to spare.
3. Regard any feelings within you, and keep your focus on your breath as you imagine these scenes.
4. See yourself boarding the plane and settling into your seat, falling back into it in the same way in which you're sitting in meditation, supported and comfortable.
5. If panic or anxiety creep up, tell yourself "I am safe" as you inhale for 4 seconds. Tell yourself "I am at ease" as you breathe out for 8 seconds.
6. Visualize yourself meditating on these phrases in your seat on the plane, feeling calm and safe throughout the entire journey.

TALK
TO STRANGERS

Meeting new people can put your fight-or-flight response in the driver's seat. You could worry about saying the right thing or about whether or not they like you. Although it makes sense that you want to be accepted by others, if you're insecure about how you come across, you'll be focused on yourself rather than on them. Think of conversation as an art. It's a skill you can practice and learn, and one that will boost your confidence.

1. While in a sitting position, cross your arms across your chest, round your chin into your chest, and carry your shoulders forward.
2. Then, unwind out of this position, relax your arms down with your palms facing up on your lap, and sit tall.
3. Notice the difference in how you feel when you're closed and guarded compared with open and relaxed.
4. Imagine you are in a room full of strangers.
5. As you consider going up to a new person to start a conversation, check in with how this makes you feel, and embody your current open and relaxed sense of being.
6. Picture yourself striking up a conversation. Make it your job to find out something interesting about them, rather than to impress them with something about yourself. Have fun and be curious rather than worrying about appearing right or clever. Tune in to them like a radio dial, asking questions, listening, and understanding.
7. Plan to pose one question to a stranger you encounter today.

RISK
REJECTION

Opening yourself up to others carries with it the risk that they won't accept you for who you are. This is another stress for which avoidance is a common response. If you never put yourself out there, you'll never have to face the pain of rejection. However, you'll never experience the joy of a real connection either. Remember that your vulnerability isn't a weakness—it's a great gift. Learn how to open yourself up to others rather than put up barriers.

1. Take three long, slow, deep breaths through your nose, concentrating on opening your mind, opening your heart, and opening your expectations.
2. Picture a relationship or a situation where you feel vulnerable to rejection. It could be a first date or the prospect of simply sharing something with someone where you're not sure how they will react.
3. As you consider this, notice any feelings that emerge. Try putting some distance between you and any anxiety by framing it as a visitor to you rather than as something you are. "I am feeling nervous" has less power than "I am nervous."
4. View yourself raising the stakes in this relationship or in this situation.
5. Imagine the outcome is what you had hoped, and let yourself feel how good this feels.
6. Imagine the outcome isn't what you'd hoped. Let the sadness move through you without judgment. Think "I am feeling unworthy in this moment" rather than "I am unworthy."
7. Know you'll learn and grow, whichever the outcome.

BRAVE
FINANCIAL STRESS

Money worries—whether pressures in the present or fears around future losses—can keep you up at night and lead to a vicious cycle of increasing mental stress. Whatever the reason for your financial worry, a common response is to plunge yourself into avoidance, leaving mail unopened or evading answering the phone. These tactics only further build up the stress in your mind as you feel guilty for how you're handling things. Mindfulness won't fix your finances, but a perspective shift can help you see the situation clearly so that you can take back control.

1. Take a deep breath.
2. Check in with yourself and how you're feeling when you're under financial stress.
3. See your situation realistically. Are you worrying about losses that haven't happened yet? Do you understand the true picture of your financial situation? Are you trying to make decisions without all the information you need?
4. Determine what you can do, and take action. Are you avoiding dealing with your money problems? Is there anything you can do right now to improve your situation?
5. Shift your perspective and prioritize. What is most important to you? Who is all this for, and what is it for? Can you simplify things?
6. Change what you can. Don't avoid things, hoping they will go away. Have courage as you determine your options and take the next steps.

FIND THE
WAY IN FAILURE

Failure in life is inevitable, but that doesn't stop many of us from trying hard to prevent it. The thing is, failure is only a negative if you see it as final. Let it be your greatest teacher. Resilience requires being able to learn from both the positive and the negative experiences you'll face. When you feel like you've failed at something, don't wallow in self-pity or feelings of unfairness. Take responsibility. Find the lessons. Move onward.

1. With every breath you take in, sit a little taller.
2. Envision yourself walking down a path and encountering a large boulder blocking your way.
3. Take in the scale of the obstacle before you and how this makes you feel.
4. See yourself finding a way around the boulder. Picture this in detail, investigating whether you could climb it, tunnel under it, or, perhaps, hack some brambles to get around it. Focus on the way forward, not on the obstacle.
5. Imagine yourself making it to the other side. View the wide-open path now ahead of you, with the obstacle behind you.
6. Now consider a challenge you are facing where you feel as though you've failed. See if you can embody this clarity of purpose to find a way around it. See any setbacks as boulders that alter your path, but that don't prevent your ultimate progress. Take responsibility and learn from any mistakes. Welcome the opportunity to practice failing.

RESOLVE
RELATIONSHIP CONFLICTS

On the one hand, a healthy, supportive relationship can make you feel capable of anything. On the other hand, difficulties in a relationship can take enormous reserves of energy and be a major source of stress. You can't control the people you are in relationships with. You can only control how you identify and express your own emotions and needs, and how you respond to the other person's feelings. Conflict is inevitable in any relationship and is not always easy to resolve, but effective communication can help.

1. Stretch your arms out wide and then give yourself a big hug, before resting your arms in a comfortable way.
2. Notice how any conflict you're dealing with is making you feel.
3. Think about the source and significance of the conflict in more detail. Is this a day-to-day argument, such as who did the dishes last, or is it an intimacy-based need not being met, such as a friend being unavailable during your time of distress?
4. Identify any unhelpful ways you might be responding in this relationship, such as avoiding confrontation, putting up barriers, pushing someone away, or surrendering to the other person.
5. Return to your feelings and what they're telling you. Try this way of phrasing: "When X happens, I feel Y, and I need Z instead." Name what you feel so you can see it clearly, express it, and deal with it.
6. Make a plan to communicate how you feel in this relationship.

MARRY YOURSELF IN SICKNESS AND IN HEALTH

It's true what they say—if you don't have your health, most other concerns of life fast become unimportant. You might be worried about an illness limiting you in the future. You could be dealing with a health crisis forcing you to slow down now. Or maybe you're fighting with yourself over something chronic that you can't control. Whatever the worry, listen to your body and befriend it—including its limitations—so that you can be at peace while you handle what you need to when you need to.

1. Scan your body where you sit, starting from the crown of your head and working down through your chest, arms, abdomen, hips and seat, and legs and feet.
2. Notice anywhere in your body that you sense any aversion or feelings of sickness.
3. Concentrate on these areas. If there are several, focus on them one at a time. Notice any sensations you associate with your health anxieties. Observe how, when you really focus on these physical sensations, they ebb and flow rather than stay steady. Breathe into the spaces of the fading of the sensation, however subtle.
4. Send relaxing energy to any spaces you are focusing on. Relax your skin. Relax your muscles. Relax your joints. Relax your organs. Relax everything.
5. Find gratitude for your body, as it is, here and now.

CHAPTER 11

MEDITATIONS TO BE MINDFUL IN THE EVERYDAY

Mindfulness is about more than the time you spend sitting in meditation—it's about cultivating a sense of presence throughout your daily life. When you're in tune with your body and mind in the present moment, you can respond more and react less to the stress or anxieties that you experience. Try these ideas for bringing mindfulness into daily moments to lower your reactivity and continually draw yourself inward to what you're experiencing in the present.

WAKE UP
WITH INTENTION

Is your phone the first thing you reach for when you wake up? Before you're even out of bed, you might be losing your mind to notifications, emails, and the endless stream of information on your device. Try this "morning pages" writing meditation from Julia Cameron's *The Artist's Way* to clear away the cobwebs and calm any anxious or stressful thoughts as you start your day.

1. Gather a pen and paper or notebook. Don't be tempted to do this on a device—you need to create the physical connection from your mind to your hand to the pen to the paper.

2. Write down whatever is coming to mind. Don't overthink it. Don't force anything. Let go of needing to be profound or useful or interesting. At the start of your day, your mind is waking up. Get out of your own way for this exercise and see what is really occupying your mind first thing in the morning.

3. Be mindful as you write, taking satisfaction in each stroke of the pen, and each word emptied from your mind onto the paper where you can release it.

4. Write until you have filled at least three pages.

5. Recognize how you feel. Now that you have emptied your mind onto the page, you can leave these thoughts where they are and get on with your day.

PRACTICE MINDFULNESS FOR 2 MINUTES EACH MORNING

Routines can be helpful. When something becomes a habit, you don't need to devote so much energy to it. Engaging in something that doesn't require much of your direct focus makes these routine moments lovely times to access peace.

But if you're prone to ruminating in anxious thoughts, the default mode of your brain that engages in these moments could be reinforcing stress rather than releasing it. Let this time of body relaxation also relax your mind. Being mindful in an everyday moment can help you challenge any negative patterns and use your habitual routines as a time for settling rather than ruminating.

1. Before you brush your teeth in the morning, set a timer for 2 minutes.
2. Notice every sensation in your mouth as you brush: the taste of the toothpaste, the feel of the bristles on your gums, and the sound of the brush against your teeth.
3. If your mind wanders during the 2 minutes, take note of what you're thinking about. Are you ruminating on something that is over and done with in the past? Or are you thinking about your to-do list and the day ahead? Every time thoughts grab you, take note of what they are, and then guide your attention back to the present experience of brushing your teeth.

LET YOUR MIND WANDER IN THE SHOWER

Have you ever noticed how many great ideas you have in the shower? It's almost like you subconsciously know that when you're showering you can't possibly be getting anything else done, so you might as well daydream in tranquility. We're obsessed with productivity in our modern lives and constantly feel like we should be doing more. But there's little you can do under the spray of a shower except wash yourself. Your mind is totally free to wander. Pay attention to this process and take it with you to the rest of your day.

1. As you stand in the shower, tune in to the present moment.
2. Engage all of your senses in this experience: the scent of your shampoo or bodywash; the sound of the water spraying from the showerhead; the feel of the water cascading down your face and body; the sight of drops merging and mingling on the wall; the taste of clean water in your mouth; etc.
3. Let your mind wander and simply allow thoughts to come and go. If any ideas come up that grab your attention and you find yourself becoming caught up in a particular story that causes anxious feelings, come back to your senses of smell, sound, touch, sight, and taste.

TAKE A PAUSE
AT RED LIGHTS

In a way, you are more likely to notice and pay attention to the negative things in life rather than the positive. Think about the times you were frustrated to hit several red lights in a row, cursing what bad luck you were having. But can you recall the last time you noticed how easily you sailed through a string of green lights? It makes sense—negatives are more likely to impact you and prompt you to take action, such as to find a shortcut so you're not late. Noticing the positive can take more conscious effort, but it's important to balance out the negatives you note with an acknowledgment of the good stuff. The next time you're gifted with a forced pause at a red light, take this opportunity to savor the moment.

1. When you're stopped at a red light, notice your breath.
2. Stay alert, watching the traffic and the signal ahead.
3. Breathe in with gratitude for this pause in your travel. There is nothing else you need to do in this moment but watch and wait.
4. Breathe out any worry about rushing or being at your destination. Consider that you're simply early for your next green light.

WAIT
WITH PATIENCE

Life includes a lot of waiting, whether it's waiting for the bus, for someone to show up, or for a web page to load that seems to be taking forever (or over 5 seconds!). Waiting is frustrating. It feels unproductive and like a waste of time. To avoid these uncomfortable feelings, we distract ourselves or become stressed and overreact to the actual situation. But the difference between patience and impatience is simply perspective, and you can choose a perspective that makes the inevitable wait times in life more pleasant than frustrating. Within this experience is an opportunity to practice a powerful in-the-moment mindfulness exercise.

1. Next time you have to wait, resist the impulse to indulge in distracting behaviors like pulling out your phone.
2. Notice what you're feeling. Name the feeling. Is it impatience? Frustration? Boredom?
3. Don't try to push away the feeling; investigate it instead. What is the source? Is it really the situation in front of you, or is there something deeper that it represents, like being out of control or stressed with time pressures in other areas of your life?
4. Scan your body and notice any areas where you're holding tension.
5. Take a deep breath, sending the breath to any areas in your body that you've identified with the feeling. Repeat for five breaths.
6. Relish this pause that you've been given to wait and experience your mind and body in this moment.

MOVE
YOUR BODY

Exercise is one of the best things you can do that benefits both your body and your mind. When you're engaged in physical activity that gets your heart rate up, you tend to be fully immersed in the activity itself. Your mind becomes focused and free, and you don't even have to exert much effort to control your thoughts, because all of your energy is going toward the movement.

1. Start with just one thing. One push-up. One jumping jack. One sit-up. One minute of jogging in place. If you see exercise as a chore, or if it's difficult to get motivated, start small. Start with just one thing so that you can have a non-zero day. A non-zero day is a day where you take at least one action toward your goal, no matter how small.

2. Notice how once you start something, it's easier to keep going. You're now on the ground, so you might as well do two sit-ups. Two can become ten. Don't decide in advance when you'll stop.

3. Forgive yourself if it is only one action today. Congratulate yourself that you did more than zero today.

4. Over time, adjust your thinking about what zero means to you. If you manage to do one of something consistently, that one becomes your new level zero.

5. Be mindful as you exercise and enjoy it. Relish that congratulatory feeling—take it with you throughout your day with satisfaction.

TAKE
A BREAK

If you spend much of your day at a desk or on a computer, it is vital to take breaks. Staring at a screen strains your eyes. Sitting down all day, although it feels like a restful posture, makes your body stiff. It's so easy to get caught up in work and to feel like every minute is needed to accomplish that one thing causing you stress. But the more hurried you get, the more mistakes you make and the more time you need to spend correcting them. You need rest. You need breaks. Take them regularly and guilt-free.

1. For about every hour you spend at a desk or in a chair, plan to take a 5-minute break.
2. Silence your phone and lock your computer during that time.
3. Stand up.
4. Raise your arms up overhead and take a big long stretch.
5. Bend to one side and then the other, stretching through your side body on each side.
6. Roll through your neck.
7. Pause for a still moment. Rest your gaze or close your eyes. Notice how it feels to be disconnected for a while. No one can interrupt you through your phone or computer. Nothing is pulling your attention away from this moment.
8. At the end of your 5 minutes, gently blink your eyes open or lift your gaze and refocus as you sit back down to focus on your next task.

SIMMER DOWN
WHEN COOKING

When you're anxious, you might constantly seek to rush through the process of things to get to the end result. You want to check things off the list as fast as possible. But there's so much pleasure to be found in slowing down as you do things. Do you really save much time when you rush? What do you lose in the experience when you do so? Try preparing a meal for yourself with mindfulness to simmer down your need to rush.

1. Prepare your ingredients. Notice the color of everything you're about to cook in its raw form. Take the time to smell each item. As you wash, chop, grate, peel, or otherwise prep, be present in these actions. Feel the texture of everything. Listen to the crisp crunches and pops.
2. As the ingredients are cooking, inhale the different smells. Notice how the individual smells change as everything combines. Watch how the colors might change as things cook, when warmed and combined with other ingredients. Hear the sizzles, hisses, and bubbling sounds.
3. Take your time through each step. Arrange the finished meal on a plate with care. Watch the steam rise and evaporate into the air.
4. Finally, dig in!

SAY NO
TO SOMETHING

Requests come to you all day. Have you ever stopped to consider whether you should be saying no to more of them? Do you feel you have to "do it all" to please everyone else? If you feel guilty and stressed about the amount that's on your plate, the next time someone asks you to do something, take a breath and consider this little exercise.

1. Contemplate what this request is actually asking of you. Is it your time? Your energy? Your expertise?
2. Think about what you will gain in return for this request. Is it even something you want? It's not always about tit for tat, but if you're always saying yes, it will harm what you can give sustainably in the long term. Will it strengthen a relationship or lead to further opportunities? Will it be fun? Will you learn something? Assess this exchange in light of what you can give in this moment. Give freely when you can, but protect your own energy too.
3. Ask yourself if you need to do this or if you even want to do it.
4. Ask yourself if it's something that is important to you. Remember that often what's urgent takes your attention first, but what's urgent isn't always what's important.
5. Practice saying no to things. Notice how it makes you feel.

CREATE
A RITUAL

When you make a cup of tea, you can simply throw the bag in some hot water and squish it against the side of the cup, and your brew will be ready in a few seconds. The result can be fine. But is the rushed process enjoyable? These little moments can be opportunities to create mindful rituals in your life. There is so much beauty in the everyday things that normally get taken for granted.

Create a small ritual for yourself. Maybe it's in your daily tea or coffee brew. Maybe it's in savoring a bite of chocolate after lunch or a skincare routine before bed. Whatever it is, take the time to enjoy it and perform it like a craft without rushing it. Try these guidelines to create a tea ritual:

1. Prepare some hot water, then pour it into a mug containing a tea bag.
2. Watch how the water changes color as it fills the mug.
3. Take the time to let the tea brew naturally. Continue to watch the water change as it deepens to a rich color and becomes more opaque. Watch the steam rise up from the mug, dancing in the air, before evaporating.
4. When the tea is ready, savor your first taste, noticing how satisfying the flavor is for not having been rushed.
5. Consider how you can take this sense of being unhurried and relaxed with you into the rest of your day.

CLEAR
THE CLUTTER

Physical clutter can contribute to the mental clutter you feel when you're stressed or anxious. Leaving dishes out reminds you of chores that need to be done. Accumulating stuff you don't need or want can overwhelm you. Try these tips to be more mindful of the clutter around you.

1. Try the rule of five. If you see something that needs to be done and it will take less than 5 minutes, do it now. Perhaps it's washing up your breakfast bowl rather than leaving it in the sink, or perhaps it is simply making your bed. When you see a task, ask yourself if it will take less than 5 minutes—don't think anything else about it—and if the answer is yes, do it without further thought.
2. During your day, be aware of anything that needs to be put away or taken from one place to another as you move from one room to the next, and take it with you.
3. When you contemplate purchasing something new, ask yourself if you can afford it. If you can afford it, ask if you will use it. Picture this thing in your life. Do you need it?
4. Play the minimalist game. Every day for a month, get rid of one thing you no longer need or haven't used lately.

For each of the previous exercises, take the time to notice how it makes you feel to release the physical clutter around you.

DRIFT TO SLEEP

Sleep time can be a very difficult time if you're struggling with chronic stress and anxiety. If you've dealt with insomnia in the past and find it hard to get to sleep or if you wake up often in the night, you can approach bedtime with fear about the experience ahead. And these problems compound—lack of sleep over time has similar impacts on your brain as being drunk and is linked to increased negative thinking patterns. Try this routine if you're having difficulty getting to sleep.

1. Go to bed at the same time every night. Consistency helps you to fall asleep at the same time and regulates your daily rhythm.
2. Create a mindful wind-down routine for yourself. This will help to tell your body you're preparing for sleep. Brush your teeth with mindful intention, read a few pages of a book, or do some gentle stretching.
3. Don't panic if you can't get to sleep. Remember you've been in this situation before and you can tolerate it.
4. Pick a broad topic in your mind, such as animals, fruits, or countries. Begin to work through the alphabet in your mind, identifying an item in the category for every letter, starting with the letter *A*. For example: Apple, Banana, Clementine...
5. If your attention wanders, keep bringing it back to the list. If you make it through the full alphabet, choose another category and start again.

CHAPTER 12

MEDITATIONS TO SURRENDER TO OPEN AWARENESS

Earlier meditations in this book focused on cultivating your attention on a focal point and using meditation as a tool to challenge negative patterns and build positive qualities for greater well-being. This final chapter is about building your own self-guided open awareness practice. With a receptive, curious, and regular personal practice, you can settle your mind both within meditation and in your day-to-day life. You're still being present, but you are no longer dominated by yourself or your experiences and are instead open to a wider conscious-ness and connection with the oneness of everything.

CREATE
A COMMITMENT

The more you learn and the deeper you go into your mind, your body, and your being, the more you might realize just how little you know and how much further there is to go. As the proverb says, "The sea gets deeper as you go further into it." Like most things worth doing in life, your meditation practice requires commitment, patience, and persistence. Start your unguided practice with this meditation and return to it whenever you feel frustrated or feel as though it's a struggle to find the time for yourself.

1. Set aside 15–30 minutes in your day to dedicate to your self-practice.
2. Before you settle into your meditation, notice how you feel about it. Is it a chore or is it enjoyable?
3. If your perspective is negative going into it, take a minute to check yourself before entering your meditation. Can you find the joy in this still, quiet time you've decided to take for yourself?
4. Affirm the following to yourself: "I am persistent in my efforts. I am patient with the process. I am committed to my practice."
5. Start your timer and begin your meditation.
6. At the end of your meditation, check in again on how you feel.

SETTLE
INTO SERENITY

A common misconception about meditation is that you are trying to get your mind to go blank. You might often be instructed to empty your mind, but you might be confused as to how to do that. The thing is, your narrating mind will chatter on whether your observing mind pays it much attention or not. So it's less about stopping all thought and more about letting it run in the background, like when a TV that you're vaguely aware of is on in the other room, but you're not really paying attention to the show. This is why, in the beginning of a meditation practice, the first skill to learn is presence through continually bringing your attention back to a focal point when you become caught up in thought. It's normal if this requires effort to do even later in your meditation practice, but over time you might find you can spend longer in open awareness without getting distracted. Try these steps:

1. Tune in to your breath.
2. Notice your inhale through your nose and your exhale through your nose.
3. Return your attention to your breathing whenever a particular thought of your narrating mind has grabbed the focus of your observing mind.
4. Do not judge yourself for having to guide your awareness back to your breath again and again. This is the purpose of meditation. You are building skill in focused attention and increasing your ability to separate your two minds.

COUNTER RESISTANCE
WITH ACCEPTANCE

If you're struggling to let go of a thought in meditation, it can be tempting to try to force it. But this doesn't work. Control leads to tension. For example, try not to think about kittens. Are you thinking about kittens now? Of course you are. When you try to force something out of your mind, it takes hold instead. Instead of resistance, try acceptance. This is a tricky thing when it comes to difficult, painful, or negative things. Think of accepting to be more like *allowing*. Acceptance doesn't mean that things are okay, that you weren't hurt, or that you should stay in this state of being forever. Rather, it means you are getting out of war with it. Because when you're in conflict, the thought will grip you harder. The good news is that acceptance is simpler than resistance—though simple doesn't mean easy! It's about releasing energy in accepting surrender rather than expending strength in a battle.

1. If a thought arises that you struggle to let go of or accept, sit with the thought for a moment.
2. Unleash your inner kitten. Imagine pouncing on the thought like a kitten would a ball of string.
3. Practice embracing the thought in full acceptance with this unbridled jump as you squeeze the thought with both arms.
4. Notice whether the strength of the thought to pull you has lessened.

RESPOND RATHER
THAN REACT

Remember, the narrating mind is greedy for your attention. This can make you react to the emotions and thoughts that it brings up, especially when these involve stress and anxiety, which trigger your need to act fast. But you have a choice about how you answer the narrating mind: reaction or response. A reaction is fast and automatic, coming from your fast thinking processes. A response is deliberate and considered, stemming from your slower thinking processes. Practice taking a pause to choose to respond rather than react in your meditation, and build a skill that will help you react less to stress in your daily life as well.

1. Tune in to your breathing, noting the rise and fall of your breath in your body.
2. As thoughts arise, watch them as if you're watching an unfolding story on a screen. Let them be whatever they are, without trying to change them, push them away, or judge them.
3. Breathe in for a count of 4 seconds.
4. Breathe out for a count of 6 seconds.
5. After this 10-second pause, investigate each thought. Think about the facts of the situation. Is the thought or emotion helpful? If it can't change what you're dealing with, is it useful?
6. Discard what doesn't help you. Plan to act on what is useful. Return your focus to your breath.

Take this pause, reflection, and choice to respond rather than react with you outside of meditation whenever stress arises.

DEAL WITH INTENSE EMOTIONS IN MEDITATION

If strong feelings swell up as soon as you close your eyes to meditate, your practice can feel impossible. Remember in these moments that intense emotions could be coming up because you've given yourself permission to listen to and feel them rather than suppress them. It might not seem like it, but this is a good thing! Negative, powerful feelings don't mean meditation isn't for you. It means you have things within you that need to be allowed to consciously surface. If the feelings are too intense, release only what you can, and come back when you're ready to go deeper, bit by bit.

1. Allow any intense emotions that come up during your meditation to be there. You don't need to let them go, push them away, or judge them.
2. Name the feelings, but rather than saying "I am...," say to yourself "I am experiencing feelings of..."
3. Know that you're safe where you sit to let these feelings move through you. These feelings are not bigger than you are, though it could feel like it. But whatever the source of the emotion, you've been through it. You can feel through it now.
4. If it is too much, come out of meditation and write down the thoughts causing the intense emotions or anxiety. You might want to carefully burn the page with a candle or lighter when you're finished to symbolically release it for now.

EMBRACE THE
DIFFICULT GUIDES

Allowing intense feelings to come up is a start, but what do you do with them once they've arrived? Try holding what you're feeling with love. Think about what Rumi wrote in the poem "The Guest House": "The dark thought, the shame, the malice, / meet them at the door laughing, / and invite them in. / Be grateful for whoever comes, / because each has been sent / as a guide from beyond." From difficulty comes meaning. From struggle comes self-understanding. Hold these difficult guides with understanding and love.

1. Imagine the feeling you are experiencing as someone who is knocking at your door. Open the door. Who is visiting you today? Name the feeling.

2. If you're struggling to name the emotion or if it is a general anxiety, take an inventory of your thoughts. Sit back and watch *them* arriving, knocking one by one at your door. The thoughts could be someone in your life, a place, or a situation.

3. Notice how you feel when each thought or emotion arrives. Invite them in to sit down. Listen to what they are trying to tell you.

4. For anything strong that you're trying to resist, just allow it to be here with love. See it clearly and hold it with understanding. As you do so, can you notice any changes in the intensity of what you feel in your body?

5. Open the door and show your visitors out when they've said what they came to tell you.

CLAIM
YOUR POWER

The path to open awareness isn't necessarily about eliminating negative feelings, stress, or anxiety. Think of it more as changing how you relate to these experiences that are inevitably going to be part of your life. The problem isn't the thought or emotion—it is in identifying with it as if it were "true" or as if it were part of your identity. Practicing "non-identification" with the swirling contents in your mind can give you perspective, personal power, and peace.

1. Notice any thoughts or patterns that come up repeatedly in your meditation and that consistently take your attention.
2. Investigate these thoughts and how you identify with them. What do they say about you? Are these thoughts caught up with your ego and your identity?
3. Imagine what it would take to release the hold these thoughts have on you. If they are something you're resisting, what would happen if you let them be part of you? If they are something you can't let go of, what would it cost you to release them?
4. Remind yourself that thoughts happen. They don't have to be accurate or true. They might not be useful or helpful. You don't have to identify with them. They don't have to say anything about you as a person.
5. Watch your thoughts as you would a show, without getting wrapped up in their content. See your thoughts, feelings, and impulses as passing events.

REMEMBER
THE GOAL

As you build your own meditation practice, it's common to enter what can be referred to as a valley of frustration—a low point where you're not sure your practice is "working" or doing much for you or where you question whether you're doing it "right." It can help to remember that meditation is less about what you experience within the meditation itself and more about how it adds calm and less reactivity to your life outside of meditation. Whether you leave a session in a bubble of bliss or you feel it was like wrestling with a monkey, don't judge the experience itself. You're doing the work to move from effortful doing to effortless being.

1. Notice how you feel after a meditation session.
2. When you encounter a stressful situation in your day, notice your response. Are you able to be aware of the stress or anxiety arising in the moment? Does this awareness translate to how you choose to respond or react? Are you better able to recognize what you're feeling and express it effectively? If you aren't meditating regularly anymore, do you notice old patterns resurfacing?
3. Consider meditation to be like going to the gym for your mind. You need to go consistently for a baseline level of maintenance. It's not a cure and then you're done. Be mindful of the positive impacts your practice brings to your life in order to motivate yourself to keep going.

END
EXPECTATIONS

You can't know where you're going when you begin this journey into yourself. You can't decide in advance where your destination is because this is a process of discovery and growth. Without self-exploration there is no self-knowledge. And without self-knowledge there is no freedom. Much suffering comes from expectations of the way you think things should be or how things should go. When things don't go as you'd expect, disappointment results. Drop the expectations and foster patience—with the process, with meditation, and with your life.

1. Observe any thoughts that come up in meditation about frustration with the process.
2. Identify the underlying expectation of this feeling. Where do you feel you "should" be by now?
3. Consider whether your expectations are realistic. How will you know you're making progress? What's a realistic time frame to see the results you hope for? How will you know if you're on track?
4. Challenge yourself to fall in love with the unknown. Love the fact that you don't know where you're going. Love that things aren't going as you expected. Love that you never end up where you think you will.

LOSE YOURSELF
TO FIND NO-SELF

As you begin to realize that your narrating mind will run on its own default mode and that you don't have to identify with your thoughts and feelings, it's natural to wonder what's left. You might be used to thinking of yourself as having an inner "CEO" running the show— a self at the command center. This might start to look fuzzier with meditation. The concept of no-self is part of the essence of open awareness. It's a frightening concept and a freeing concept at the same time. Explore this concept when it starts to be less effortful for you to hold your focus in meditation—when you begin to really deepen your meditation practice.

1. During your meditation, watch the beautiful, strange, wild stories in your mind unfold.
2. Listen to your steady, constant heartbeat full of life in your chest.
3. Feel your breath fill you and empty you.
4. Let your wants, desires, and impulses come and go as passing events.
5. Allow the rich images and sensations from all of your senses to dance around and within you as they pass.
6. Experience them all as they dissolve. They'll stop being so big in your awareness as you move into effortless being, a state outside of all these inputs and information. You're not pushing them away, but they're flowing without your involvement. There's no "self" or commander at the center of it all. There is only open, spacious awareness.

DETERMINE
YOUR PURPOSE

A sense of purpose is critical to living a good life. It's so important, in fact, that psychiatrist and Holocaust survivor Viktor Frankl identified it as a key to surviving the concentration camps. Feeling aimless is a horrible feeling and a cause of existential anxiety. A sense of purpose helps you sort through your experiences, situating the negatives in context, and helps you more quickly recover from any acute stressors. Try this mindful journaling exercise when you need to reconnect to a sense of something larger than yourself.

1. For thirty days, at the end of each day write down in your meditation journal what brought you joy that day. Be as specific as you can. It might help to try to notice any moments you experienced "flow"—where time seems to fly by as you're engrossed in what you're doing.

2. After thirty days, review your notes, and notice any patterns: Does your joy come from interacting with others? From helping? From working on deep work? From creating art? From being physical? If you're struggling to see a pattern, ask yourself why a particular thing brought you joy. Ask "Why?" five times and you should get to the root value that is important to you.

3. Identify how you can dedicate more of your life to what brings you joy—and less to things that deplete you.

TAKE THE
RIGHT ACTION

Sometimes meditation can feel too inward-focused. After all, you exist in an environment and a culture, and it can seem like mindfulness is all about ignoring these very real contexts and their systemic limitations. Focusing on yourself could even be demotivating and breed passivity. While it's true that many things are out of your control, meditation isn't about inaction. It's about seeing things clearly so that you can take the *right* action.

1. Meditate on something in your life where you feel you lack control or influence.
2. Thinking of this situation, notice how you feel. Perhaps it's a feeling of unfairness, anger, or upset.
3. Investigate where you feel this in your body. Notice any areas of pressure and strain.
4. Examine your efforts here in relation to the situation. Are you resisting the constraints and fighting the obstacle? Are there ways around it? When you hold it and see it clearly, where is the place you can start to go around it? What first step can you take? Do you need persistence? Or is it a case of knowing when to quit?
5. Release any baggage you hold on to that clouds how you see this issue and makes you feel too helpless or disadvantaged to view clearly what action you can take.
6. Ask your heart what the best action to take next is. Your heart might not know how to get to the end goal. But it knows the next step.

BE
AT ONE

Build your open awareness self-guided practice bit by bit every day—going into yourself, but also realizing as you do that everything is connected and that you are a part of it all. You are made of stardust. You make space and the universe breathes you in. This final meditation is a beautiful Sanskrit mantra that embodies the oneness of everything.

1. Either to start or close a meditation session, repeat the following mantra to yourself out loud: "Lokah Samastah Sukhino Bhavantu."
2. Reflect on the message of this wish, which in English means "May all beings everywhere be happy and free, and may the thoughts, words, and actions of my own life contribute in some way to that happiness and to that freedom for all."
3. Hold this wish for yourself before radiating it out from your heart to your loved ones, widening the circle to include everyone you know, and expanding even further to include everyone and everything.

INDEX

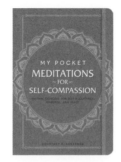